Seeds of Change

Triage for the Soul

Seeds of Change

Triage for the Soul

Eva Suzannah

AYNI
BOOKS

Winchester, UK
Washington, USA

First published by Ayni Books, 2012
Ayni Books is an imprint of John Hunt Publishing Ltd., Laurel House, Station Approach,
Alresford, Hants, SO24 9JH, UK
office1@jhpbooks.net
www.johnhuntpublishing.com
www.ayni-books.com

For distributor details and how to order please visit the 'Ordering' section on our website.

ISBN: 978 1 78099 473 4

Design: Stuart Davies

Printed and bound by CPI Group (UK) Ltd, Croydon, CR0 4YY

We operate a distinctive and ethical publishing philosophy in all
areas of our business, from our global network of authors to
production and worldwide distribution.

CONTENTS

For Mia and Kasper

Desiderata

Go placidly amid the noise and haste, and remember what peace there may be in silence.

As far as possible, without surrender, be on good terms with all persons. Speak your truth quietly and clearly; and listen to others, even to the dull and the ignorant, they too have their story. Avoid loud and aggressive persons, they are vexations to the spirit.

If you compare yourself with others, you may become vain and bitter; for always there will be greater and lesser persons than yourself. Enjoy your achievements as well as your plans. Keep interested in your own career, however humble; it is a real possession in the changing fortunes of time.

Exercise caution in your business affairs, for the world is full of trickery. But let this not blind you to what virtue there is; many persons strive for high ideals, and everywhere life is full of heroism. Be yourself. Especially, do not feign affection. Neither be cynical about love, for in the face of all aridity and disenchantment it is perennial as the grass.

Take kindly to the counsel of the years, gracefully surrendering the things of youth. Nurture strength of spirit to shield you in sudden misfortune. But do not distress yourself with imaginings. Many fears are born of fatigue and loneliness.

Beyond a wholesome discipline, be gentle with yourself. You are a child of the universe, no less than the trees and the stars; you have a right to be here. And whether or not it is clear to you, no doubt the universe is unfolding as it should.

Therefore be at peace with God, whatever you conceive Him to be, and whatever your labors and aspirations, in the noisy confusion of life, keep peace in your soul.

With all its sham, drudgery and broken dreams, it is still a beautiful world.

Be cheerful. Strive to be happy.

(Max Ehrmann)

Foreword

It is a pleasure to write the foreword for this amazing little book.

Eva shares in an honest un-patronizing way with the emphasis being on recovery to restore well-being: our rightful state. Her positivity shines through and her quirky style makes it an easy read. She writes in a clear, positive way and you are getting advice all the way through.

If life is squashing you in a suffocating way, it can be hard to know where to start or how to begin to recover your balance. *Seeds of Change* takes you gently by the hand and guides you through a variety of processes that are simple to try out.

On a daily basis I come across people who have lost their way and believe happiness belongs to others. Just reading the rules of happiness may well change your life.

If you are suffering – read the book.

If you're not suffering – read the book.

If you aren't happy – read the book.

If you're happy – read the book.

A small package that delivers big results. I guarantee that you will nod, smile and probably say to yourself, 'Oh yes.'

I'm off now to be wabi-sabi.

Enjoy x

Barbara Ford-Hammond – author, publisher, therapist and muse.

Introduction

Reflective Voices

'I feel so empty, there is nothing there. There is no one there. I feel so completely alone and abandoned. They can't reach me; it's like I'm in a different world, another dimension. I'm exhausted; everything feels hopeless.'

'I hated being around all the do-gooders, people who tried to cheer me up all the time. They really annoyed me. Suggesting things I should do to snap out of it...take a holiday, go to the gym, learn to meditate, read books or have a massage. Didn't they understand that I simply didn't have the energy for any of that? In the beginning I was so weary it was an effort just to get up in the morning and get through the day. I didn't feel like socializing, I just wanted to crawl into a corner and lick my wounds. I felt broken.'

'It's been two years since I had my breakdown. Two hard, demanding and upsetting years that I wouldn't be without. They have taught me so much about myself and my life. I think that is the most important word – life – and I decided that I wanted to live it. No matter what the outcome, life is to be lived. When I think back to that time and compare it with where I am today, there is a huge difference. Looking back like that makes me feel happy and really sad at the same time. I think I feel grief...grief that I went through so much sadness and pain, spent so much time feeling really bad and sad about myself. Just feeling really, really bad. Sad that it took me so long to understand that I was somehow living light years away from myself, *me*. When I think back on who I used to be I'm not sure I want that person back and then sometimes I really miss parts of me and my life...and feel so sad deep inside.

I do feel happy though, that I survived such a difficult time in my life and came through OK. Happy that I have family and friends who love and support me; people I can talk to. I'm really excited about all the things I have learned along the way, the energy I feel. Like having a zest for life and a feeling of adventure, not taking so much for granted anymore. Perhaps the word that best describes how I feel is Humble – about me and my life. Perhaps Gratitude is better...happy that now I know what's important and what isn't. It's easier to be myself, more comfortable. It's fun being me.

Some people tell me I was lucky to find you, and perhaps I was. But most importantly, I feel proud of myself for having done this. I've done it my own way, at my own pace. Everyone needs to find their own way at their own pace. I am convinced that anyone who goes through the process discovers a better way to live life.'

I don't want to be a do-gooder. I don't want to annoy you.
I do want to give you some tools, some food for thought.

I know that a lot of people felt life took on a new and better meaning after using some of the methods in the book. A lot of hearts healed along with those who discovered the seed of contentment, peace and happiness inside; they learned how to live life as themselves.

Doing everything at once is overwhelming and reading this book cover to cover can cause too much confusion if you want to incorporate the exercises as well – where to start? The introductory chapters set the scene for you, so it's a good idea to read them through. When you're done and have spent some time thinking about how great you are and the choices you now have, my suggestion is this:

Browse and trust your intuition. When your eye catches something that stirs you, read it and then do it. When you're done, you'll feel different. Better, calmer, more in control. More you.

Not making plans or having goals can be really refreshing sometimes; to do things for the pure pleasure of doing them. Play and make discoveries, be an intrepid explorer, be the map-maker of an extraordinary land and erase the white bits where it says 'Here Be Dragons.'

Repeat from the browsing bit and change happens in such a gentle way you just flow with it all. Ripples on a very beautiful pond.

1 Mind-Body Medicine

Let me introduce you to the most amazing, effective, gentle, awesome, natural and simple healing tool on the planet:

Your body and your mind

When they work together, supporting each other harmoniously, you'll experience the effortless joy of optimum health tingling from the tips of your toes to the top of your head and everywhere in between.

Dr. Candace Pert discovered cell memory and that communication between mind and body is a two-way street, whereas before it was assumed the brain sent commands to the body that would silently obey and never answer back.

Meditation became mainstream, Jon Kabbat-Zinn taught us the importance of this very moment – the only one we have – and the body responded beautifully to this and other mind tools.

We pondered the fact that people who have some form of faith and those who believe in the power of prayer recovered faster after surgery, healed better and could return home sooner than those who said they didn't have faith in anything in particular. The question was:

'How can this be?'

It's a long answer that is still coming. Yet it's all so simple, it's just that we complicate things, but if you start with this simple fact:

The purpose of your life is to be happy, to be enormously, fantastically happy – to the point where you need to take a sharp intake of breath from time to time because the whole thing makes you giddy – and then, if you have time to do other things, consider that a bonus for being good with lifetime time management.

Herbert Benson, MD at the Benson-Henry Institute, has been a shining beacon in the field of Mind-Body Medicine, and has encouraged many to open their minds and look at the scientific proof available for what was once seen as Eastern rituals; not quite right for the Western world where we have pills for such things.

Their work is based on the absolute connection between the mind and the body – the complicated interactive communication that take place between thoughts, the body and the outside world. Mind-Body Medicine combines modern scientific medicine, psychology, nutrition, exercise and belief to enhance the natural healing capacities of both your body and mind.

When you understand how this works, you can take responsibility for your well-being and health. Self-care and self-nurturing become the most natural things to do.

Between 60% and 90% of all visits to a doctor are for complaints that are stress related; some cancers, heart disease, diabetes, asthma, obesity, infertility, chronic pain and gastrointestinal disorders are just some of the problems that could have been prevented or the effects of them lessened with Mind-Body Medicine.

Many of you have at one time or another come across the comment: 'You're just trying too hard,' which, although well meant, is probably one of the most senseless things to say. Although in connection with stress, it's just about right.

Instead I'd like to say:

You are not present in the moment, not present in the present and not present in your body. You are most likely somewhere in the past, re-living failures or disappointments, or somewhere in the future, constructing a disastrous outcome for your most heartfelt wish – but hope springs eternal and fearsome worry becomes part of it.

It's not that you're trying too hard; you're trying in the wrong time zone.

Stop trying and start doing and being and when you do, the results will be different and I think you will be pleasantly surprised.

Mind-Body Medicine is miraculous – and the miracle is you.

You are more than capable of increasing t-cells to boost your immunity, lowering your heart rate, blood sugar, blood pressure and stress response with your mind. What's more, you can also make muscles relax in seconds, strengthen and align bone more effectively, heal injuries quicker, and the possibilities on the emotional side are endless; actually we are just beginning to discover them.

Let the journey begin!

2 Introducing Stress

The meaning of the word 'stress' has changed to include the reasons that you feel stressed. Originally, 'stress' meant the reaction that happens as a result of pressure or perceived threat (the fight, flight or freeze response) like lack of time, debts and the consequences of not meeting deadlines. In everyday language 'stress' is used to explain a state of being – 'I feel stressed.' In scientific terms there is no consensus as to what should be included and what it actually means, so I thought it might be a good idea to clarify some of it.

The Brain Rules – OK?

Stress is different for everybody. What you see as a breeze can be experienced as extremely stressful by someone else and vice versa. Some cope with the sight of blood, others faint. Some people climb Mount Everest; others get dizzy standing on a chair. It's all in the mind and it's all about how we perceive it, so when someone tells you they feel stressed, they mean it, even if you see the situation differently.

The human mind is also unique in its ability to predict future events – like lying awake worrying about things that may or may not happen tomorrow.

'Coping' is the process of interpreting and reacting to situations. Your ability to cope can be reinforced by an increase in material, psychological and social resources. There also growing evidence that people who are physically active and well rested find it easier to cope with or avoid stress reactions. If the brain interprets a situation as threatening, the fight, flight or freeze mode kicks in and the body will be in a constant state of alertness. Usually this is exhibited in behaviour, often as irritation or hostility and the person can become very defensive. How many times have you been told 'You're over-reacting'? Or how many times have you said it to someone else?

Over a period of time, stress reactions like these often develop into something more serious – a feeling of 'giving up' or feeling down, being more subdued and emotionally exhausted.

The factors that can lead to psychological and physiological stress reactions are stressors. Anything from an external crisis to a physiological strain can be a stressor. Normally, stress happens in the various social settings we live in – work-related issues or personal relationships.

Physical Reactions to Stress

How the body reacts to stress also starts in the brain. Neural systems that control our digestion, stomach and intestines as well as muscle and pain reaction are activated. When you cope better with a stressful situation the activation lasts for a relatively short period of time and your body resumes a more balanced function. If you find it difficult to cope, the activation becomes a constant state of alertness and physical symptoms become more evident – sore muscles and an aching back because your muscles never relax; a racing heart-beat due to the higher levels of adrenaline being released into your bloodstream on a constant basis. Your internal organs suffer the strain and become damaged.

Tipping the Scale

As everything else in nature, your body relies on a finely tuned balance. The human body is truly amazing but despite its resilience it has limits.

When you suffer stress for longer periods, your hormonal system changes – the imbalance causes physical damage that in some cases is irreversible. High blood pressure, heart attacks, high cholesterol, obesity, diabetes and cancer can often be traced back to stress. And though there is no cure for diabetes, there is an easy cure for stress.

Not One Reason But Many

With our modern lifestyle, illness doesn't always happen for only one reason. There are many factors involved in why symptoms and illness develop – and it can take years between the symptoms developing and you actually noticing a difference. Modern life is a risky business for your body. On a cellular level, very little has changed since our ancestors crawled out of the sea, climbed up a tree and then came back down again. Science and technology move forward in giant leaps but our bodies remain constant. In the past 400 years, the only thing that has changed in the human body is that in northern Europe, people are more able to digest cow's milk. So a change in lifestyle may be beneficial for you when you have to face your own version of a saber-toothed tiger!

Taking Control of Your Wellness

Of course there are a whole lot of things that make you stressed that you have no influence over – but there are ways to cope differently and better with them. There are also things that you may feel you can't change – but you could influence others to change (constructive communication is a wonderful tool). Then there are the things that you definitely can change, even if right now they are beyond your comfort zone. You don't have to change your life completely in one week – change one small thing every week. You will notice a difference. If the word 'exercise' conjures up pictures of fitness training, aerobics and sweat, remember that walking for 30 minutes a day is exercise. It makes you feel better, breathe easier and sleep better. You also lose weight, become more flexible and stress becomes something you more easily can take in your stride.

Chain Reaction

Modern living is confusing for the body, not to mention the brain. In a joint effort to ensure your survival, any stressful situation floods your system with adrenaline and cortisone. Which is really good if you intend to physically work off the effects they have on your body – for instance running away or fighting an adversary.

Proteins are called up from your thymus and lymph glands to form sugar for more energy, so your blood sugar level soars in a matter of minutes. Because modern stress seldom relies on us to expend physical energy to work off stress, the excess sugar in your blood is stored in your liver where it's converted into fat and when needed can be released again as sugar. So you put on weight or become obese (this is only one factor contributing to weight gain).

Abnormal amounts of salt are retained, so your blood pressure goes up. Minerals, especially calcium, are taken from your bones, and after every instance of feeling stressed your body tries to repair the damage caused – you might say 'one step forward and two steps back'. If you eat a balanced nutritious diet, exercise regularly, practice some form of stress management technique and have a good work/life balance, you're less likely to suffer any long-term effects of stress. BUT, if you do suffer from stress, chances are that at least one of those elements are lacking in your life. Here is what happens then:

Your thymus and lymph glands become totally depleted and shrivel up, so protein has to be found elsewhere in your body. Primarily, this will be taken from your kidneys, liver and stomach wall. Stress really does eat you from the inside – as is the case with stomach ulcers and ulcerative colitis. As an example, if you have a day of continuous stress you'd need to drink nine pints of milk to replace the protein you'd lost, in addition to replacing the amount your body normally uses for everyday function and maintenance.

I'd like to highlight the fact that it's not only emotional stress that affects your body. Here's the start of a downward spiral: a cold or other physical illness is also stressful for the body, and emotional stress makes you more vulnerable to colds.

Even things like an x-ray can damage (stress) your body and there is an increased need for proteins, linoleic acid, minerals and vitamins. Similarly, drugs (whether prescribed or recreational) damage your body. Here's an interesting little fact for you: if you smoke, you probably know that the brain releases endorphins when you smoke, which is why smoking seems to reduce stress. But endorphins are natural pain-killers and that's why they are released when you smoke – to lessen the pain you'd otherwise experience when you inhale smoke. Remember the first time you smoked? The burning sensation you felt? Without the endorphins you'd still feel the same now as then.

Using the 'one step forward and two steps back' analogy, sooner or later your body reaches a stage of exhaustion, it has no more reserves and more serious illness occurs. By the time you have reached this level of stress you are less likely to recognise that you are, in fact, seriously stressed. Others around you may mention it to you and it would be advisable to pay attention.

Did all this information make for gloomy reading? Then read on for a happy ending!

First, take a moment to think about the enormous capacity your body has for healing itself. Then, take a decision to look after it better. Moving out of your comfort zone always feels strange at first until the new habit becomes the comfort zone. Make changes in small steps; that way you're more likely to stay the course.

In its early stages, when you are more aware of it, stress is much easier to manage and take control of, so don't put on a stiff upper lip and think that you are less of a man or woman for admitting to problems with coping. It's so easy to think 'I'll manage' but now you know that even if your mind may think so, your body knows different. Stress management is an investment in health and well-being.

Start thinking about how you would like your life to be and remember that actions speak louder than words.

Sex and Relationships

Stress is one of the most common reasons for loss of sex drive, because it is associated with the fall in testosterone and estrogen levels, and the rise in the level of prolactin, a hormone which has a powerful negative effect on libido – it literally switches off sex drive and reduces fertility. So, stress lowers the sex drive, and a low sex drive in a relationship causes stress in itself, which creates a rather vicious circle. That's the physical side of the matter.

Emotionally, there are several reasons why a low libido occurs in a person who feels the effect of stress:

A stressed person finds it difficult to relax (partly due to the adrenaline levels) and allow the kinesthetic centre of the brain to take over.

When the sex life in a relationship becomes (almost) non-existent and the matter isn't addressed, the likelihood is that arguments will start between partners.

In addition to the arguments ensuing, the stressed partner is also likely to suffer from exhaustion, irritability and guilt – the latter will most likely make the person act in a defensive (aggressive) manner.

Comfort eating can easily lead to obesity, and a person who has gained a lot of weight (particularly a woman) may feel that she is unattractive and loses libido in a form of self-disgust.

Never giving purposeful time to be with a partner can also create problems, and learning to set aside intimate time together (that does not have to include sex) will improve matters.

Stress and Fertility

Let's go back to the comment 'You're trying too hard.'

When you try too hard, you become frustrated, stressed, tense and most of all, you don't enjoy it any more (whatever it is you try too hard to do).

At Cedars Sinai in Los Angeles, and in other places, a lot of research is going on into the connection between stress and fertility. At the present time it's rather elusive; although there is a clear connection, they're not sure exactly how it works. Stress hormones have a lot to do with it as do the feel-good hormones. When you feel good your blood flows easier so some proteins connected to implantation are enhanced. Increased blood to the uterus impacts conception.

Your blood ph-value plays a role as well; when you're stressed, your blood is more acid and fertility is compromised. IVF treatment is less likely to be successful, which starts the stress cycle again.

When you start using relaxation techniques and stress becomes manageable, even if you haven't been able to conceive before, your chances of being successful are greatly increased.

There is one other thing you can do daily that will counteract the blood acidity:

try some apple cider vinegar in hot water, and add a little honey if you prefer. Take 1 teaspoon, three times a day. If you eat red meat take the vinegar after the meal. Red meat is pure protein and when you digest it; your blood becomes very acid. It will help all round to work this habit into your daily routine. It may not be practical for you to carry bottles and jars around with you every day, but you can get bottles of ready mixed honeygar or capsules of concentrated vinegar from health food stores.

If you carry too much weight you could be pleasantly surprised by the effect this has on you – and be a few pounds lighter.

The Flipside of Stress

We usually associate stress with pressure, lack of time, work and demands, but there is the other side of the stress-coin: boredom. Not having enough to do, or being bored with what you do is just as stressful, only less noticeable.

When you comply to please others or want to reach a goal but the distance between A and B seem impossible, stress levels rise.

Compliance is the family dinner you didn't want to go to, but your mum/aunt/grandmother would have been upset if you didn't go.

When you say you feel great when you actually feel less than OK, tension and stress builds up, because your brain gets confused over the discrepancy between words and feelings.

The unattainable goal is easiest illustrated by the person who wants to lose weight. If you wear size 20 and would like to fit into a size 14, but do nothing about actually losing weight and instead all you do is procrastinate while wishing you'd fit into the size 14 – you will feel huge amounts of stress. You would probably counteract this by eating, adding to the mounting weight produced by stress itself.

There is an Awful Lot of Good Stress as Well!

Challenges that make you feel alive and excited or your ability to cross a busy road without running into a bus; winning races and the feeling of being on top of the world: this is also stress.

How you perceive situations makes a big difference to stress levels and how you cope with them.

If you have ever done something really scary and exciting, like a parachute jump, the feeling of fear before the jump is exactly the same as the feeling of excitement you feel a fraction of a second after the jump, but your perception has changed.

I know that you have your own version of the parachute jump; courage is subjective and always worthy of deep respect.

Finally

I know this chapter delves into the far reaches of how your body and mind react to stress, but browse the pages, pick up the information that interests you the most and leave the rest. Perhaps you'll have a renewed interest in the remainder when you notice how good you feel after using any of the methods for stress reduction and relaxation.

Isn't it brilliant that such a complex issue is one of the simplest to deal with? Ten minutes of deep relaxation boosts your immune system, and a good laugh, a genuine feeling of love or a warm hug flood your body with endorphins, healing you, making you feel positive and stronger.

How fantastic are you to do all this without even really trying? So the possibility that you can do and be even more isn't that far-fetched.

Go on, amaze yourself!

3 With the Mind in Mind

Many of the exercises in this book ask that you pay attention to mind and body in the moment. Mindfulness is a form of meditation, practiced for thousands of years in the East and is a fairly recent concept to the rest of us. Usually when you experience negative feelings – fear, frustration, anger, guilt, anxiety or pain, to name a few – your mind immediately fights the feeling, tries to avoid it or ignore it. A mind version of sticking fingers in your ears and singing la-la-la, because just about all of us spend much of our lives trying to feel better or happier or both. We also spend far too much time avoiding things we don't like, mourning things we've lost and regretting things we've said. The lifelong quest for the elusive feeling of happiness that's always just out of reach leaves us with unanswered questions like, 'Why me?' or 'Why don't I feel better?' Happiness, like mindfulness, is something that needs to be experienced rather than talked about – and if we stop running ahead and become aware of the present, we would be much closer to feeling happy. The same goes for feelings of contentment, peace and satisfaction; you know all the positive feelings you could have but are too busy looking for them to experience them. Two things happened when I first started meditating mindfully: firstly, I realised how much my mind had wanted something like this to happen – like when you take a sip of cold fresh water and realise how thirsty you are. Secondly, when I found those precious moments of stillness, I felt nothing but total love and happiness. Perhaps that's the hardest thing to realise, that it was there, hiding inside you all the time. It's also extremely personal; your journey of discovery is unique to you and your life, it follows only your road.

Awareness, attention and remembering are the three keystones in mindfulness. Being aware of what's occurring within and without is powerful enough in itself because then you can start to separate yourself from difficult feelings, thoughts and emotions; and when you start paying attention to your awareness, you're even more empowered. The third aspect is that of remembering but this doesn't refer to things in your past; it's a reminder to pay attention to your awareness. A fourth aspect that makes it more complete for us in the West is that of acceptance. So, for example, when you practice just paying attention to your breath, the mind will wander off. But the moment you notice and bring it back to the breath, you remember to be aware and instead of feeling that you somehow failed, you accept that minds have a habit of wandering; you give yourself praise for remembering to be attentive to the awareness of accepting it.

Similarly, if you have a problem or emotional pain you want to be free from, you will be more successful in doing so if you first accept the problem. When you hold it at arm's length, fighting to keep it away, you'll never quite understand the problem and so it's difficult to be free from it. At best you'd be able to push it a little further away, but sooner or later it's there in your face again.

Meet Metta

Metta is best translated as loving-kindness, towards yourself and others. Being kind to yourself is perhaps not the easiest nor the most comfortable way of living, for two reasons: self-love and self-kindness are judged as being selfish, arrogant and oblivious to the needs of others. Secondly, there is much emphasis put on berating ourselves – to learn from mistakes, we all make them and after all, we're all just humans; we could do better, wish for the past to be different and the future to be gloriously wonderful because right now we sit here, passively wishing for it to be so. But without an effort on our part to change or do or be anything other than full of wishes it's not likely to happen.

So be loving-kind to yourself – for every action you feel bad about, I bet you can find at least seven others that prove you to be a kind, generous compassionate person. A thought, a smile, a single word can make a lot of difference and you just forgot to look on that side of the fence. Then, do the same for others; reading this book and doing some of the exercises will make it all less daunting. By others, I mean all other humans and creatures, in fact everything on and including the planet. Just as you strive to feel happier, they do too. Things look different and I promise your life will feel very different when you grasp the fact that you are not alone in feeling worry, loneliness, fear, anxiety, pain or sadness. Right now, randomly, take the fourth person you see and spend a few moments understanding that they too feel and think the eternal quest questions. The second step, to feel compassion for a person you dislike, are afraid of or feel jealous of will come in time, when you have learned to love yourself with more compassion.

It brings things into perspective in a world where good news just doesn't sell newspapers. It's worth remembering that there is an awful lot of good news, we just forgot what it sounds like. We don't even choose words that are positive – even when what we want to convey is positive. If someone asks you how you are, do you answer 'not bad' or do you perhaps say 'I'm OK' without much enthusiasm? Or any of a long list of versions on the same theme? I asked participants in a workshop this question, and someone replied, 'Yes...I'm guilty of that.' Which is precisely my point – don't be; become aware and then change.

Do as I Say, Not as I Do

Imagine being able to live with openness, trust and integrity. Would your life be better, would you finally feel happier? Oh yes, I hear you say, but people...well they're not like that. People aren't kind, generous, open and honest and if you are, they'll just take advantage of you, treat you like a fool and break your heart. I'd like to remind you of the fact that they too feel, think and desire the same as you do. Besides, you're 'people' too.

If I want people to be honest and open with me, I have to be that to them, and importantly I have to be honest and open with myself. I believe we lie more to ourselves than to others and to get truth from others we need to be truthful too – at all times, not just when it feels OK. There is much to contemplate and reflect on, so many questions but right now perhaps not the courage to face the honest answers. And that's all right too. Acceptance, remember?

Being afraid or feeling confused and being able to acknowledge that that's how you feel is a greater step than you perhaps are aware of right now, but before you reach the final chapter you'll be incredibly proud of yourself.

It's not a case of Practice Makes Perfect – Practice Because You Are Perfect.

4 Making up for Lost Time

Remember those days in childhood when time seemed to stand still and a day could last an eternity? Especially if you were waiting for something exciting or important, like birthdays or summer holidays. There was so much time to spare you could have bottled it.

Now perhaps when you think back, you're living a life where time is in short supply, you never seem to have enough to finish everything on your to-do list and it's hard to believe that every day of your life has had and will always have 24 hours, no more, no less.

Your perception of time, your ability to organize and prioritize all the demands that you – and others – put on your day makes a difference. How well you feel in control of life, work or relationships makes a difference and it's always easier to carry on with the same old behavior, however stressful it may be, rather than change habits. But in reality, taking a conscious decision to change opens up new and exciting possibilities.

Taking the First Step

Get to know yourself better. Learn from experiences and mistakes and press the pause button now and then; just pay attention to what is happening right at that precise moment.

What are you good at? What aspects of your life make it run smoothly? Is there anything you can improve on, just to see if you can make it even better? Try it; if it works, great. If it doesn't, you have gained another mistake to learn by.

Knowing yourself and understanding how you act and react, your strengths and weaknesses, with honesty and acceptance – now there's an incredibly strong foundation to build a life on!

Some questions you will benefit from finding answers to are:

- Do you have a good balance between 'doing' and 'being'?
- What would you like to accomplish?
- How do you want to feel?
- Can you be more in tune with your intuition?
- What drives you?
- What's your way of thinking?
- Can you make space for mindfulness in your life?

Allowing the questions to just 'be' in your mind will encourage the answers to come to you.

Going Forward

We all attach meaning to things in life, and what is meaningful to you is your unique viewpoint. Many are driven by a wish to make a difference, leave a mark on the world and be remembered through the annals of time. If our efforts are appreciated and noticed by others, it encourages us to do even better and we all have a greater potential than we'd like to admit or even believe.

In order to go forward, to make the mark and be appreciated, we must enter unknown territory from time to time. Changing habits – good or bad – happens one step at a time, as we break away from the negative and move towards something that makes life a richer experience. In order to do that, we need to move fluently between the known and the unknown to achieve what we've set out to reach.

The comfort zone: this is where you feel at home with your habits (those that you don't even have to think about), where you can procrastinate, be bored and live on autopilot without having any real challenges or opportunities to grow as a person. If you stay in this zone, you will always have what you've always had.
    The discovery zone is where you feel excited and motivated,

challenged to use and develop your skills and talents. You can grow and learn, feel content and totally aware of how wonderful life is. Here you will discover natural passions and talents that perhaps you had no idea you possessed; but being yourself without the ego getting in the way is just the best discovery ever.

The risk zone: this is the area where you have to deal with demands that are difficult and sometimes impossible to meet. Your stress level is dangerously high and you feel the physical strain that comes from not being in control. It doesn't matter how skilled or resourceful you normally are, here you have very few resources to regain control. Most of the time you'll be in this situation for only very short periods of time – the most common one is starting a new job or taking on new responsibilities.

We move back and forth in these areas all the time; some spend more time in the comfort zone, others too much time in the risk zone – and neither offers you the opportunity to thrive in the middle.

Stand Your Middle Ground

If you imagine the zones as three interlocking rings that overlap where they connect you'd have a picture of the ideal life. If you take one step forward, all three would move, a constantly evolving life that would be infinitely rich and rewarding. Actually, this is a life worth aspiring to and one very few of us ever attain – but it's possible to get close, very close in fact. Here are some points, tools, ideas and thoughts that may help you get there:

- What's stopping you from changing?
- What's stopping you from creating and finding solutions?

If your life was a film and you were the director with free reign to create what you'd like:

- What type of film would it be? Adventure? Thriller? Romcom? Musical? Fantasy? Comedy?
- What's the film title?
- What's the theme that runs through the film?
- What life events would you film?
- What important milestones would be the highlights?
- What actor would take the part of you – and all the other characters in the film?
- What message does the film convey?
- Is it a Hollywood blockbuster or alternative film?

Habits

How aware are you of your habits? Good or bad, get out of autopilot and pay attention to the things you do out of habit. What is your ingrained reaction to stress and pressure? As your awareness grows you'll come up with new, fresh solutions and become more positive both in thought and deed. How would your hero or heroine in the film change things for the better?

Changing the habitual things for something different can be quite cathartic – like viewing something familiar from a different angle.

- Take a different route on your daily journey.
- Read a book on a new subject or in a different genre.
- Have a make-over, new style or new colors.

How does it feel to do something different, something out of the comfort zone? Notice the change in yourself and also what effect it has on those around you.

Time Check

When it comes to habits and time, we all have a favored way of behaving – always being early, always being late, wasting it, procrastinating or delightfully always being on the dot. Our own time habits and those of others can be irritating and frustrating and ultimately very stressful. It can seem like a trap that it's hard to get out of, so practicing new habits in different areas will help you to get a grip on time.

If you:

- always meet a deadline
- see the whole picture
- have a solid structure
- enjoy planning and organizing
- like things to be 'just so'
- produce work that is meticulously exact and detailed
- work better on your own rather than in a team
- demand perfection from yourself

Then:

Don't be so hard on yourself, you don't have to be perfect all the time. If you always strive for and achieve perfection, where's the fun in that? It's also a lot of pressure, always having to live up to your own standards and judging others by those standards as well – nobody is ever good enough, not even you.

Take one moment, sit back and close your eyes. Breathe in. Breathe out. Give yourself a break, give yourself permission to relax a little, expect a little less and appreciate yourself for the person you are, not the impossible perfectionist you think you have to be. Self-worth doesn't come from being flawless. It happens when you start accepting who you are and believe that flaws make you look particularly fantastic.

Then again, perhaps you're not aiming to be perfect, you could be:

- very optimistic about available time
- generously giving away or wasting your own time and that of others
- seen as irresponsible and disorganized
- certain you can complete a 30-minute task in a fraction of the time
- completing things – but hardly ever on time
- bursting in to meetings gasping for breath
- precariously juggling too many balls at once

I bet you have a favorite excuse – or a really well-rehearsed way of coming up with new and ingenious ones. I also bet you feel frustrated with your time-keeping, disappointed in yourself because you know everyone else in your life feels let down by you.

For just one day, write down every excuse you use and give some thought to which one commonly occurring thing that you made an excuse for (again) you can change. Late for the bus, train, school run, work? Late getting back from lunch, getting to a meeting, or even getting home? Pick only one and put all your altering efforts into changing it for the better. You'll feel great for it and those around you may be pleasantly surprised. It's such a good feeling you may even want to do it again...and again.

You may of course be nothing like this, instead you're

- carefree happy to enjoy the little things that make life worthwhile
- 'being and experiencing' a lot more than 'doing and accomplishing'.
- living in the moment, taking each day as it comes
- an advocate for any slow-movement; ie slow food or slow

travel
- creative and full of ideas that never materialize

When those around you lose their... I think someone else has already used that line. Just don't minimize the stress those around you experience!

If your life is full of unfinished projects, or there are things you avoid completing, perhaps now is a good time to find out what the resistance is all about? Maybe there is a deeper reason, something to discover and resolve. What stops you from taking responsibility and completing projects? Can you see yourself taking a step back, smiling, and with a feeling of total satisfaction, saying, 'There, it's finished.'

The Fallen Hero

Always striving for perfection, always getting things done on time whatever the cost comes at a price. Sooner or later the urge to wave a white flag at life becomes impossible to resist. Give up, capitulate, the fight is over and you lost. You think. The truth is that if you demand perfection from yourself all the time, or if you find yourself in a job where the demands are too much, you will:

- feel lost and disoriented
- feel like a victim
- have abandoned or forgotten your own needs
- feel apathy and despair
- wonder where time disappeared to
- be very close to mental exhaustion
- need help to start believing in yourself again

Ask for help or accept it when offered to you. It may be a bitter pill to swallow when you have been capable, independent and very strong for a long time, but now is the time to hand over to others, to delegate. In time you'll get closer to understanding that asking and accepting in this situation is strength of a human kind, and is particularly kind to humans.

Write. A journal, a note, a list of feelings or experiences. Just write ... worries and things that made you want to scream. Moments of calm, feelings of happiness or being safe. Note any aches and pains, where they are and why they are there. What makes you tired? What gives you energy? If everything is chaos in your mind and you can't decide which word to write first, here's an effective way to decide:

- Do nothing.
- Breathe in, count one, one, one while breathing.
- Breathe out, count two, two, two.
- Continue until you reach ten, ten, ten.
- Take a nice deep breath and write the first word that comes into your mind.

As you develop the skill of being still in your thoughts, spend one minute doing nothing, with no goal in mind. Breathing in and out with ease – does it make you restless or is calmness spreading in you and around you like a soft blanket? Does one minute seem like a second or an eternity? Persevere and eventually you can expand the practice to two minutes; then you can spend one minute doing nothing and one minute thinking about things that make you happy.

All the Time in the World

Occasionally you encounter someone who seems to be perfectly balanced, they:

- are seen as a role model
- have a healthy work-life balance
- always have just enough to do, never too much or not

enough
- are always busy but never stressed or under pressure
- take responsibility for their own deadlines
- make decisions based on what is realistically possible

Do you recognize yourself? Perhaps it seems like an impossible dream, to manage time so well; at least some of the time you're in control.

So when you meet someone who's even more in charge of their own time, ask them how they do it. What's their attitude to time? How do they keep cool and balanced?

Changing is being brave enough to pause and reflect on who you are and who you'd like to be; how you spend your time and how you'd like your life to be. Being totally honest with yourself, what really matters and what can you let go of? To have a good work-life balance you need to pause and reflect from time to time, to take stock. Being aware of your needs and taking responsibility for how you manage your time put you in control. Then you'll move back and forth between the circles, with easy flexibility. Sooner or later someone will come along and ask, 'How do you do that?'

24

Working, eating, sleeping and daily routines take up a big chunk of the allotted 24 hours, but what would you like to do with the rest? What would really enhance your life, make it rich and rewarding? Here are some questions to start you off:

- Is time valuable to you or do you let it slip through your fingers?
- Are there moments when you're aware of being alive – and of savoring every second?
- Do you ever waste it when you feel you could be using it better?

- Do you feel you have enough, too much or too little time for the things you want to do?
- Is there anything you'd really like to do if you could fit it in?

Now that you have a clearer picture of your time, how well do you feel you're in control of it? On a scale from 1 to 10, where 1 is no control at all and 10 is total control, where are you right now? Does it surprise you or were you aware of where you're at? What would your life be like if you were closer to 10? What could you do to gain more control?

Things to Consider

There are circumstances in our lives that we have no control over but we can change our attitude towards them. We can also become aware of what we're asking of ourselves and become more reasonable and realistic. Are people or circumstances in your life realistic and reasonable in their demands on you? What about your demands on them? Are you reasonable and understanding or a hard taskmaster, impossible to please?

It's not always evident that time management is at the root of dissatisfaction or stress. Habitually we apologize for being late, forgetting things, not managing to do all the things we said we'd do – shopping after work, cooking dinner, picking up kids, going to parties, having lunch...and I haven't even started on the little things at work. Or the important, big ones at home and at work. Probably best not to even mention demands from friends and family, or the things you'd really like to do yourself. Because we all do the same – put our own needs last while busily trying to please everyone else. It's time to change, time to live your life for you, doing more of the things you love.

Here, There and Everywhere

Let's take this very precise moment when you're reading this. Evoking all your senses, feel the book or reading device in your hand; the weight, the smoothness or texture, how it feels and fits in your hand. What sounds do you hear? A breeze rustling through the leaves of a tree, raindrops on a window or a bumblebee humming? Cars driving by, people talking or birds singing, someone mowing a lawn?

A few other things that are delightful to notice: the taste, texture, sound and smell of an apple as you bite into it; the fresh juice in your mouth as you notice the color of the apple – the shades, shape and patterns.

Being aware of time, being mindful, gives more meaning to your life. It stops you from:

- wishing you could go back to change mistakes you made
- worrying about things that haven't happened yet
- feeling bitter about people who hurt you in the past
- letting your mind wander when someone is talking to you
- thinking that things will get better – some day, later, next year...
- feeling irritated about little things that don't really matter
- always trusting your head and never your intuition and heart
- carrying on until you're exhausted, both physically and emotionally
- feeling that everybody's out to get you
- ignoring the subtle details in life
- having sleepless nights
- feeling dissatisfied

Instead, you forgive yourself and others, sleep well, have goals and plans that move you forward, have energy and love life, trusting that your choices and roads are the best for you.

Don't be so hard on yourself, stop judging and start just being. Let thoughts come and go; let them flit through your mind like dragonflies on a still pond, darting all over and disappearing from view, then flying off to another pond. Thoughts and dragonflies aren't good or bad here, they just are, so let them be without attaching meaning to them. After a while, it happens that when the last dragonfly moves out of view there is a moment with just a still pond. Enjoy it! Soon thoughts return, but with time and practice there will be more moments with just a still pond and they will last a little longer. You are the pond with no ripples.

Exercise: Imagine That

Make yourself comfortable. Sitting in a favorite chair, lying on a bed or a sofa, just make sure you feel relaxed, that your body is supported so you can feel cared for just now. When you're cared for, you can let go and think about other things, experience other things. Feel sensations that you're normally not aware of because you're too busy doing this and that. But right now, you can breathe a sigh of relief, knowing that you don't have to even think about this or that, you just have to be comfortable, cared for, letting everything else go, letting your eyelids close. If you put your hands on your cheeks you can feel the warm skin against the palms of your hands, and the slight pressure of the hands on your face. Just feel how perfectly your face fits into your hands and notice the shape of your face. Your cheeks and your lips, the contour of your chin as you trace the line of your eyebrows with your fingertips. Just be aware of the sensation, the feeling of being you. Awareness of who you are, your existence and place in the world; your presence in the present. Your importance, even if you think you're just a dot on the map, because you are unique and your space in this world was reserved so that you could come here and do what only you can do. And you could only be here now, in the present, to do what you are here to do. It couldn't have been in the past, or in the future, only at this moment. It's a little amusing and completely unfathomable, how the universe planned your place, in among all the others, all the things that needed to happen and all the people you had to interact with to get to this very moment. Even more fantastic is that you did it – without stress or worry that you should get here on time or that you'd have everything ready before now. You had just enough time and will always have just enough time to do the most important thing of all – to live your life.

5 Can You Hear What I'm Saying?

This exercise can be done with a partner or a friend – it's a useful tool for all relationships.

Arrange uninterrupted time for your sessions – at least 20 minutes.

Eliminate all distractions, remember to switch off your phones. This is planned intimate quality time so treat it as special. There should be no eating, drinking or smoking during the session, it's not a snack break. The point is to create sacred space and be as mindful and aware as possible.

Determine whose turn it is to start (alternate between sessions). Divide your time equally. I suggest using a timer or alarm so that you can totally devote the time to talking and listening without keeping an eye on the clock.

The speaker says whatever he/she feels like saying. It can be about anything, including the events of the day, feelings from the past or relationship issues. Avoid conflictual subjects or those you feel anger or resentment about, as well as blaming and 'you' statements such as 'you don't understand me'. Use 'I' statements such as 'I feel alone.' The speaker must use up all his/her time even if it is just to sit in silence.

The listener's job is to simply listen with eyes, heart and 100% attention. The listener is not to respond or talk for any reason.

When the speaker's time is over, switch roles. Remember, the new speaker is not to use his/her turn to respond to what the other person has said. This can be saved for the next session.

It's liberating and empowering to be able to speak your mind without being judged or having to weigh your words carefully so as not to upset or hurt the other person. As the listener, your focus should be on the other person, and your thoughts only on the words they speak. Most of the time you're more likely to be focusing on how you're going to respond, or reacting emotionally because you assume it's all about you. Learning to respect that what a person says is about them, not you, makes for wonderful relationships. No blame, no guilt and no assumptions, just deep respect, understanding and trust.

Exercise: Imagine That

Sitting in a favorite chair or standing in your favorite room, pick one point to focus on.

Make it a point somewhere above eye level, perhaps where the wall and the ceiling meet or a corner of the room. Now find a specific point and put all your attention on that spot.

As you do, your field of vision narrows down, as if your eyes have become a camera lens. Pay attention to every detail contained in the spot you picked; notice everything about it.

It won't be long before you realize that this actually takes a lot of effort; it's quite a strain to focus on one spot like this. So when you feel ready to stop, just let your eyes relax, and feel all the little muscles around your eyes begin to relax.

See what happens then? Your focus softens and your vision expands. Suddenly, you can see much more of the room, from the ceiling to the floor; you'll even notice textures and colors all around you. Your peripheral vision grows wider and your breathing relaxes. It eases and slows as the vision grows.

When you're ready you can stop paying attention to your breathing and the ceiling and just look straight ahead, staying just as relaxed as you are now.

Instead, you can pay attention to any sounds you hear – in the room, outside the room, on the street or in the garden. Just ordinary, everyday sounds. And the more you hear, the more you see when the two merge and hearing becomes seeing.

How does this feel? Perhaps you can imagine that inside you there is a ball of glowing light, and if you can, you'll also be able to imagine that the light from the ball shines through you, out into the room. Feel it now? A warm, tingling light filling your inside and outside. And when the light beam touches the wall or the furniture, imagine what it feels like to touch it. Feel the texture in your mind; imagine the feeling of smooth or rough, hard or soft. Warm or cool.

As you see it, get a sense of feeling it and hear the sound your hands and fingers make as you touch it.

In this moment you will have total awareness, total connection with whatever you focus on. You will also have total relaxed calm awareness, on the inside and on the outside. Comfortable control, when thoughts slow down and after a short while become so still your mind will be silent.

Enjoy it and know that you can return to this state anytime you want to.

6 Vision Boards

Before the concept of vision boards emerged, you were encouraged to write affirmations and stick them on suitable surfaces around your home to remind you of the goal you wanted to reach. The theory was that if you looked at the affirmations often enough, you would start to believe or act in accordance with the desire.

I'm sure they were effective for some and probably highlighted emotions for many, but the fleeting glimpse of 'I now truly respect my body whatever shape it is' and any anxiety felt were probably never connected.

Mind mapping is another tool used as an aid to get from A to B, identifying challenges or obstacles, solving problems or finding inspiration. Trouble is, I was never good at map reading. When I see a mind map, I switch off, assuming it's a diagram showing how wires are to be connected. But I guess it is the best description, a map showing how the wires (neural pathways) in your mind should be connected for best results. Great as this may be, I am still not connecting.

Bearing in mind that women are right-brained, holistic and able to see bigger pictures, you may find that a vision board is a better tool of discovery. I certainly did.

Making a hands-on real board is a work in progress, one that can highlight a lot of internal issues that you may not have been aware of before. Shapes, patterns, words, poems, pictures of houses, cars, take-away menus or fluffy cats. So why collect all those bits and pieces when you can just cut and paste images onto a screen?

You can get a real feel for what is meaningful to you by touching all the different textures you put on the board. Wood, fabric, paper, shells – whatever you place there, you have a feeling for. The same happens with the colors you are attracted to and add to the collection – they speak volumes about you and now is your chance to listen.

Your vision board represents all that is you – make it from whatever material you feel is most appealing to you – perhaps a large colored poster card, a piece of cardboard, wood or a white-board. It's like having a display of feelings, statements, memories both good and bad; one that is a constantly changing visual statement. Write what you feel will have purpose, or draw something, and add color, texture, pictures from magazines or photos.

As the board grows, something very interesting happens while you spend time arranging it – feelings, thoughts and words will come to you. Perhaps memories from the past, emotions that can be quite strong and usually very surprising, will surface. Pay attention to your thoughts, and as these things come to light, you will see with more clarity and resolve previously hidden obstacles that perhaps hindered you. If fear or sorrow have been lurking in dark corners, you can deal with them and let them go, because these emotions are not relevant to your present life. Instead you can fill the space with good positive energy.

You can use the exercise in Letting Go, or any other imagery that feels right for you. It's also a perfect time to be in the moment, mindful of how you feel.

As this is truly a work in progress there will be times when you realize that a piece on the board isn't needed anymore, or you want to represent it in a different way as you work through emotions and come to understand aspects of yourself and your life. The vision board will help

- you connect with the real you
- you start making choices from your heart, not your head
- you to decide what you really want to do, not what you think you *should* do
- you become more creative in your choices
- you gain clarity
- to inspire you and act as a reminder when things are tough
- you realize where you are disconnected from your true self
- you reconnect with your core identity
- old wounds to heal
- you make space for positive emotions

Hopefully as you read this you are thinking, 'It's a good idea, I might try that sometime.' If so, set a definite date for when you will start your board. You could start collecting pieces for it right now. Perhaps you'd like to make different boards for different issues or goals in your life. Until you start the process, you'll never know how healing and liberating it can be to express yourself in a visual and tactile way.

Exercise: Imagine That

If you've ever been into a forest you'll know that it's a different world in there. A different silence, although when you hear the birds sing I guess it's not so silent after all. Or the noise from the trees; the wind moving through the branches, the creaking of old wood, or pine cones falling to the ground with a muted thud. The ground where they land is covered in pine needles, twigs and perhaps moss; a carpet that softens the sound of your footsteps and there's a scent of wood and earth.

Perhaps there is a path in the wood; you can walk along it, going further in among the trees and every few steps you are in warm sunlight shining through the canopy above; the next you're in the cool shade. Sometimes it's nice to take yourself off some place where time is of no importance but your experience is what matters.

It is possible that, as you walk along the path further and further into the forest, you'll spot something on the ground, or hanging from a branch. Perhaps someone else found it and thought you'd be sure to come looking for it, so they picked it up and put in on the branch for you to find more easily.

Maybe it's something you had forgotten about, but now that you have found it, you remember how important it is and how good it feels to have it in your hand again.

So the best thing to do is to put it in your pocket and keep it safe. Now and then you ought to check that it's still there; just touch it briefly and feel how good it is to have a magical symbol all of your own.

7 Core Values

Your choice of inner values is unique to you even if right now you're not aware of what they are. They define and shape every aspect of your life and are connected to your personal identity, so if you lose sight of them, you lose sight of who you are.

Being authentic and true to yourself in life is impossible until you have identified and acknowledged them. What is central to your sense of well-being? Answering questions like this helps to access your inner drives, pinpointing what is actually important to you.

From the list below, chose 10 core values that are important to you:

Love	Marriage
Respect	Security
Power	Achievements
Health	Passion
Acceptance	Happiness
Integrity	Humor
Children	Family
Success	Kindness
Adventure	Freedom
Independence	Trust
Excitement	Honesty
Compassion	Intimacy

Once you have identified them, you need to prioritize them. Spend some time interpreting each value and what it means to you – what makes it significant in your life? Why is it important?

Which of these negative emotions would you most like to avoid?

Rejection	Anger
Frustration	Loneliness
Depression	Failure
Humiliation	Guilt

Whatever you ticked on this list determines your behavior in almost all situations – and how true you are to your core values.

Being authentic – being yourself – often means taking emotional risks and that means confronting the emotions you most want to avoid.

Pick a time, any time...

...when you felt on top of the world; when you were so happy you thought you were going to burst. Actually, think of three times when you felt happiest.

What made you feel so elated? Then look at other key moments and significant memories; perhaps a theme is beginning to emerge? It could be one of your core values making itself known.

Now think of three moments when you felt the opposite, times when you perhaps felt angry, rejected and overlooked. What made you feel that way? Your answers should be the direct opposite of your true values, so if you were bullied by someone you may have felt suppressed. Your core value in that case could be Freedom.

Make a list of 10 people you most admire, from famous historical characters to celebrities and neighbors. Below each name list the reason you admire them – traits or achievements and ideally, give an example.

Here too, you will see a pattern emerging and by now you probably recognize your own values in these themes.

It all sounds so simple, but this exercise is a really good way of clearing out all the other voices in your head – parents, teachers, peers and others who influenced you in your formative years when you were most impressionable.

Parents who wanted what they thought was best for you; teachers who delivered the curriculum and its values tainted with their own beliefs; peers who pressured you to conform if you wanted to be in their gang, who in turn were influenced by their parents…the merry-go-round of values and behavior is quite a dizzying ride, don't you think?

So what happens is that you try to please everybody, fail most of the time, and start believing you're a failure, and feeling guilty and miserable. While inside you there is this feeling trying to get your attention: your true self.

Now you need to pay attention to the person you are trying to please and realize that they are trying to please you – so now you're both miserable.

Jump off the ride, stop the game and be yourself, inside and out.

Before you even begin to protest that you can't possibly be yourself, because people might not like who you are, please re-read the page from the top.

Before you were aware of your values, perhaps you at times felt uncomfortable and dishonest, tearful, or had that nagging feeling inside. Examples abound, but common things would be to agree with friends or family on any issue, from TV shows to football teams and then to feel irritated about it and them. Or again, voting for the same political party as your parents did – even if you don't really know what they stand for and if or not you agree with them.

Another area to pay attention to is in your achievements – do you feel really proud, really happy about reaching your goals? I'm talking about that genuine feeling, not the pretend version with the fake smile and empty heart.

If you're not feeling happy to the core, perhaps you need to examine whether the goal is yours at all. Then, follow your bliss.

8 Real or Imagined

If you wonder what the future has in store for you, you don't need to see a fortune teller; you do it yourself all the time. Unfortunately, you probably just foretell doom and gloom, because that's human nature, unless you decide to tell yourself a better story about your future.

Whenever you worry about something that hasn't happened yet, your body immediately thinks it is a reality and responds accordingly. So if you're waiting for someone to turn up and they're late, you start thinking that they've had an accident – your mind starts to run riot, as you imagine the worst scenario possible.

By this point, your body is running on stress hormones and you feel really faint, wondering if you should call the hospitals, the police or just run round in a circle screaming, 'Oh my god, oh my god.' All because of something you imagined. When you lie awake at night, worrying about a meeting in the morning, you do exactly the same thing; you predict your future in the gloomiest way possible.

If you watch a film, have a dream, read a book or actually experience something, it makes no difference to your mind. It can't tell the difference. For all its clever, amazing and breath-taking abilities, it just doesn't know.

An oversight? Probably not; we're too smartly engineered for that. Instead, start thinking about what a wonderful advantage this is, the ability to pretend something has already happened, and know that your body will respond to it.

Similarly, if you bring to mind a happy moment, you feel happy. This is just as curious, considering that the event that made you happy isn't happening now. Memories of things that made you happy, sad, angry, frightened, feel in love or excited, all work in the same way.

Here's something to try: close your eyes and bring to mind a moment when you felt really relaxed, really tired in a good, cozy way. Remember when you snuggled up safe and comfortable (this may be a memory from a long time ago). Remember what the material next to your skin felt like; the smell; if it was day or night. Can you feel how that same sense of comfort is working its way through your body? Your mind is already there, so this is a great shortcut to produce positive changes.

If you have been in a trance, for instance, you can easily go back into a trance at any time by recalling what it felt like, or simply by imagining that you are in a trance again. If you haven't, just recall what it feels like to daydream and you get the idea.

The last aspect I want to mention is the one about self-fulfilling prophecies. I'm sure you have recognized some of the things I have mentioned so far, but this one is more elusive, harder to grasp and perhaps to accept. We subconsciously act and behave in such a way that what we predicted actually happens. Then we can say, 'See? I told you so.' When there was a bird 'flu scare in the UK, I was working in a large office. One morning we were handed a list detailing the symptoms of the 'flu and told to go home if necessary. Within two hours five people had left – their imagination had made them experience symptoms of bird 'flu. They returned to work the following day, feeling absolutely fine.

This book is full to the brim with ideas and tools for you to use to change bad to good – for good.

Not only that, but the changes you can make will happen on a deeper level, where true belief lives. I don't know if you have met before, but let me introduce you to:

The Chattering Monkey and Your Subconscious Mind

You think around 5000 conscious thoughts every day. Thoughts that you are aware of to a greater or lesser degree, from focused concentration to where your mind wanders off into surreal and strange rooms, or just wondering what to have for dinner tonight.

In contrast, the real controller, your subconscious mind, thinks around 95,000 thoughts – and they really count and make a difference. The 5000 on top make little difference to your beliefs, behavior and choices; it's just a trick your conscious mind plays on you. I sometimes think of the conscious mind as a real jobsworth receptionist, who is ineffective, misguided and standing in the way of contact with the real decision-maker.

As an example, using fMri (functioning magnetic resonance imaging) on a smoker, shows that the subconscious mind decides to smoke almost a second before the conscious thought appears.

How you speak to yourself internally makes a big difference externally. It's the stick you beat yourself up with, it's the voice that stops you from having fun, makes you feel guilty and prevents you from reaching phenomenal heights. The good news is that you can stop the chatter and gain control with positive self-talk.

Stick your tongue out and gently hold the tip between your fingers. Relax for a moment and notice that your mind goes quiet.

Because mind and body work together when you think, tiny muscles in your tongue move. When you stop this from happening, your mind quietens down. Not a very practical demonstration and people would probably look at you with singular fascination if you did this in company, but placing the tip of your tongue against the roof of your mouth just behind your front teeth has the same effect.

Using visual images or imagining things works as well:

Imagine or visualize the 'chattering monkey' (or a nervous kitten or puppy) and gently stroke it, soothing it to calmness.

Visualize or imagine a volume control, a slider or a dial and turn down the volume on the voice inside.

Try different things, experiment and see which method works best for you. There is also a possibility that while you play with this, your own version appears and will work better than any of my suggestions, and be vastly more effective!

A curious thing happens when the inner voice is calm; you listen better and hear what is actually being said with a new clarity. This is especially useful when the talk is very emotional. The internal voice is master at 'interpreting' what is said, makes things up and generally it confuses matters.

Practice when you're relaxed and have the time and you'll get really good at this. You will notice fantastic benefits using this method on its own, and when added to any of the other tools you can really reap the benefits of it.

9 Visualizations and Guided Imagery

A well-told story can be mesmerizing; the Grimm brothers and Scheherazade could testify to that.

Your brain works in images, so painting a picture or setting a scene 'goes in' easily. Your conscious mind relaxes – because, 'It's only a story.' There is no need to think about content or trying to figure out what it all means, right?

You of course know that this is the ideal ground to sow seeds of change, and to watch them sprout and grow with incredible speed.

Just as when you agonize through the night about a meeting the following day, I hope you also tried the opposite: meditating on a happy memory. In both instances, hormones are released into your bloodstream, carrying either damaging or healing power with them.

While you may skip the details leading up to your own happy memory, guided imagery leads you gently through relaxing scenes, engaging all your senses, opening the right doors, healing the right wound.

It also helps to heal new wounds; after surgery you'll heal faster if you have used guided imagery. You'll also need less pain relievers. Clever you.

For a lot of people with disabling, chronic or terminal illnesses, guided imagery allows a degree of control, a place to breathe fully and let go of the anxiety that so often is part of life. You may experience the same – to forget just for a moment, to relax and allow peace into your life and mind. Interestingly, your mind will create symbols that represent a solution, strength, healing, comfort or whatever you need at that moment. Even when someone else guides you, your mind may well produce scenery or a single image of an object that seems totally unrelated, but this is more powerful than any image someone else could present you with. After all, it's your own subconscious image, created by your own mind which knows best and want nothing but the best for you.

One way of practicing the imagery muscle is to imagine that in front of you is a wooden chest, full of objects. Without looking, reach in and pull out the first thing you touch and see what it is. Sometimes they're useful things, other times just silly or maybe beautiful. Keep pulling things out, empty the box and start a new one. You can also pull out three objects and make a story based on them. Let your mind feed you the words; don't interfere with thoughts if it doesn't make sense – because on a much deeper level it is making sense to you.

Exercise: Imagine That

When you become still and stay in the moment, just breathing gently, you can sometimes actually feel a presence inside, of passion and love – and the more you focus on it, the more you become aware of it. You become absolutely certain of where in your body it resides; perhaps near your heart, perhaps behind your belly button. But wherever it lives it has a distinct shape, color and brightness, perhaps its own distinct sound. So now that you're in this moment, pay attention to your own energy, the love you project out to the world. Describing and visualizing it usually makes it brighter, radiating love all around you. Perhaps it has that particular warmth that makes people want to stand closer to you, so that they too can feel it. Or maybe your light shines like a beacon all across the world so that those who recognize it will come into your life and add another dimension to it. When you become aware of its place and purpose, every time you enter the light you'll be reminded of its healing and rejuvenating qualities, and as you bask in the glow, every cell whispers, 'I'm home.'

10 Tantrums at Thirty

When was the last time you were told you were behaving like a kid? For most of us it wasn't that long ago, because we do behave like children when reacting emotionally.

Tears, tantrums, wanting to stamp your feet and shout that it isn't fair – your adult self has left the room until the emotion subsides.

Here's the reason:

Your brain is like a reference library that stores information about how to behave and react in certain situations. There is a major flaw in that it doesn't update the information unless prompted, so every reference is interpreted and stored only once; the first time it happened.

Let's take two different things you learned as a child:

Birthdays were absolutely fantastic when you were a child – presents, parties, cakes and lots of attention in the best way possible. The sun always shone down from a blue sky for you. So that lovely memory is your reference to your birthday and everybody else's birthday. You cannot understand why someone should be miserable, not have a party, etc; even as you think of those birthdays, you smile and feel all fuzzy.

You told a secret to your best friend when you were six and trusted that she would keep it. Instead, she ran straight to the girl you hated and told her all about it and then they laughed at you, practically telling the whole world. No great hole appeared to swallow you up, so you just had to put up with the hurt, embarrassment and confusion. You learned about betrayal, but because it was so painful, you never re-evaluated it again as you grew up. So all your brain has as a reference is the behavior and emotion of the six-year-old girl, and you will go straight back to this when faced with a similar situation.

The sensible thing to do is to go back and re-evaluate, to look at that first incident with adult eyes and remove the trauma (because that is what it is). Most of the time you live with a greater or lesser degree of fear, wanting to avoid the pain and any situation that could possibly trigger it off.

All you normally will be aware of is the reasoning your logical mind has attached to it, just to make sure you don't have to deal with the unpleasantness of the memory, even if it is just a silly lie.

Incidentally, this is also why it takes longer to recognize that you don't know what something is, because you have no reference to it. Everything is connected to everything else.

As you learn to let go, slowly peeling away the layers, you will reach those initial events and deal with them without tension or fear. The results can be breathtaking and liberating, and your life more of a breeze, less of a struggle.

11 Take a Deep Breath

A sigh of relief, a sob or a sharp intake of breath, we breathe all the time and pay little attention to how we actually do it. Your lungs cover most of the area beneath your ribcage, and they are there to be used. Eastern traditions give a lot of importance to the breath – *Ki* is life force, because without it, there is no life.

Do you breathe into your shoulders or your stomach? Shallow or deep?

When your body is tense, you breathe in the upper region of your chest in short shallow breaths not providing enough oxygen and carbon dioxide for either your body or your brain.

Diaphragmatic breathing is overall the best; it allows for balance, health, vitality and calm. It also burns more calories and keeps your blood alkalized which is ideal for good health.

If you don't already breathe into your stomach, spend some time practicing, it will help in so many ways and certainly calm your mind before you start using the various methods in the book.

Breathing out for longer than you breathe in –this is the calming effect you want to achieve. So breathing in for a count of 7 and breathing out for a count of 11, you will relax in an instant. 7/11 may not be comfortable for you but since the main pattern is to exhale for longer than you inhale, you can chose a pattern that suits you better. 5/8, 4/7 or 6/9. It is supposed to be calming and relaxing, not an exercise in how difficult it can be to breathe.

The Relaxation Response
Relaxation is a focused state of awareness that can enhance your life on so many different levels. It lowers blood pressure, helps you cope with pain better, sleep better, ache less and generally be in a more positive mood.

Learning the relaxation response is an easy two-step process:

Repetition of a word or a sound – a mantra – or a repeated muscle movement.

When other thoughts enter your mind, just let them go with passive disinterest.

Use a word, short phrase, or prayer that is deeply rooted in your belief system, such as 'one,' or 'peace.'

Make yourself comfortable and still your body and mind.

Close your eyes.

Relax your muscles, going from your feet to your calves, thighs, stomach, shoulders, head and neck.

Breathe naturally and slowly, and as you do, say your mantra or word silently to yourself as you exhale.

Be passive, don't fight things that come to you. Don't worry about how well you're doing this – it's of no importance. If other thoughts come to mind, just say to yourself, 'Oh well,' and go back to your repetition.

Continue for 10 to 20 minutes.

Just be still and keep sitting quietly for a minute or so, allowing other thoughts to return as you slowly become aware of your surroundings. Then open your eyes and sit a while until you're ready to get on with your day.

Practice once or twice a day; before breakfast and dinner are ideal times. Not only will you feel much more at peace with yourself and your world, but it will also make the food taste better and aid digestion.

There are many different methods you can use to enable your body to respond with complete relaxation. Here are some alternatives for you to consider:

- imagery
- progressive muscle relaxation
- repetitive prayer or chanting

- mindfulness meditation
- repetitive physical exercises
- breath focus

When you elicit the relaxation response:

- your metabolism decreases
- your heart beats slower and your muscles relax
- your breathing becomes slower
- your blood pressure decreases
- your levels of nitric oxide are increased

Lastly, let's consider the easiest of them all; the passive observation of the breath, as you inhale and exhale. This is just paying attention to how it feels when your lungs fill with air, and noticing how the ribcage gently moves with each breath. No counting, no patterns, nothing but ordinary breathing. A moment when nothing else matters, when all you have to do is breathe. Feeling the texture of your clothes against your skin and your feet resting on the floor, noticing perhaps how the soles of your feet feel against whatever they are resting on. All while you are just paying attention to your breathing. In doing this the breath can transport sounds to be distant, softer and muted, and peace can expand within you with every breath. If you pay attention to the skin on your arms and the area just above your arms, you could just possibly become aware of the energy that surrounds you. A slight vibration perhaps. And while you feel that, allow your eyes to move down to your hands; let them rest on the palm of your hand. Left or right, it doesn't matter. See how the lines in your hand make shadows and patterns and as you move your fingers the shapes change. And how as you tilt your hand this way or that way the shadows fall shorter or longer, to the left or the right.

By using the breath, time can stand still and you can be at

peace – in this very moment.

I hope you enjoyed the moment of awareness in Mindful Meditation.

12 Be Very Nice to Me or Leave Me Alone

When you go through difficult times – whatever the difficulty is – and in particular sadness and grief, it's hard to accept that life goes on as normal, as if nothing had happened. Perhaps the wish would be for everyone, including strangers, to be considerate without having to ask them.

Grief, anger and guilt all have their time and space.

So do letting go, allowing light, happiness and hope back into your life.

You are not your feelings. They are something you experience, so you're not an angry person, you're a person experiencing anger. Why am I saying this? Because I believe that these two things need to be separated and once you become aware of the difference it's easier to let go and make space for positive feelings. I am not minimizing the feelings, neither am I 'awfulizing' them. Only you know how long you need to grieve, but guilt is not a reason for continuing to grieve.

Releasing negative and limiting beliefs and feelings allows you to control your emotions, rather than letting the emotions control you.

Giving yourself permission to let go of sadness, anger, grief, guilt or frustration opens the door to freedom and positive feelings.

Permitting yourself to let go of all the negatives is a process that takes place over time.

Start with small things that are good to get rid of and good to practice with.

Everything in this book is beneficial on its own and if you experiment with a combination of things you'll forge your own path, creating images, ideas and thoughts that just come to your mind.

I had a letter from a woman who had been working through her grief. She wrote:

'I suddenly knew what I had to do to let go, and I wrote it all on a piece of paper. I dug a small hole in the garden, put the paper in it and a flower bulb on top and then filled the hole. I've just been out in the garden and seen the green shoots emerging from the ground. I feel so happy, so relieved and although I still feel sad my grief is different now and I look forward to the flower growing!'

So the important thing to keep in mind is:

You are not your feelings, they are something you experience. Sometimes they are good and you feel in control, other times they are negative and run riot. Letting go is a process that brings peace and freedom, less limitations and more control.

Once you realize that emotions are an experience, it's time to understand the curious behavior we all have – that we hang on to emotions for dear life. We hang on to anger, fear, sadness, apathy and everything else, as if our life depended on it, because we believe that we are our emotions.

It's time to loosen the grip and simply choose to let go.

Sometimes, when working with clients on this, I notice the slight jolt of indignation; I am not asking you to let anyone off the hook, just to let go of the emotion and give yourself some peace.

When I started my own process of letting go, I was amazed by the amount of memories, emotions and slights that bubbled up to the surface. I could feel really angry about things that had happened all the way back in primary school; I was in my thirties and the incidents had been forgotten until then. Well, obviously not, judging by my reaction.

Remember to start with small things!

There are many variations of the process, but here is one that has worked for a lot of people:

- Set aside 30 minutes for yourself; no phones or other disturbances.
- Take a deep breath and just enjoy being able to relax, there are no demands on you right now.
- Breathing deep into your stomach, pick one situation that is bothering you right now. As this comes to the surface, you'll be aware of the tension that develops in your stomach and how it may restrict or change your breathing. Notice how it can spread into your body; if you pay attention perhaps you'll feel how every part of you tightens.
- Imagine that this tension, the tight feeling, is all gathering in the stomach (you probably feel it there anyway). Notice exactly where in the stomach it is.
- Focus on the tension; if it had a shape, what would it look like? Small? Large? Round or angular?
- If it had a color, what would it be?
- Now that the tension has a definite shape and color, make it a small enough size to fit in your hand.
- As you imagine it moving from your stomach to the palm of your hand, notice how you breathe easier, how your stomach relaxes.
- With a soft, deep breath, gently blow on the shape and watch it turn into thousands of particles, vanishing like sand. As the particles float into the air, they explode and twinkle like fairy dust.

Repeat steps 1-9 with everything and anything that surfaces. If you still feel tension over an issue that you have let go, it could be that there is another aspect of it that needs to be released.

We identify with our emotions; I do, you do and everyone else does. I am sure that at some point in your life you have come across a really strong, capable and assertive person who suddenly breaks down and you become very confused, because a strong person just doesn't do that. Or, think of someone who normally appears cold and how suddenly you see a really warm, caring side of them that you didn't even think was there.

These revelations can be confusing because you have to re-evaluate your impression. When you separate the person and the emotion you can start building a clearer, more accurate picture of yourself and others. Victims have strengths too; just pay attention to the person, not the emotion.

I believe that the reason for this emotion-driven behavior is that we respond accordingly. If instead you respond to the person, things will be easier because you cannot fix things for someone else. Neither can anyone fix your emotions; only you have that skill – now.

Depending on how stressful your life is, it's a good idea to have a regular clear-out session however often you think it's necessary. Then of course there are the almost daily irritations – someone cuts you up in traffic, a complete stranger in the super-market throws out a comment that makes you want to throttle him. Now you have two options – you can let the incident ruin your entire evening or you can take a moment to get quality and harmony back in your life.

13 Journaling

How many of you wrote a diary when you were younger? Perhaps one of those nifty things with a padlock, where you wrote about who you had a crush on, who you hated and what happened last weekend – a personal and secret record of external events and the impact they had on you.

I'll pass on the question about how many of you had siblings who tried to get into your diary and read it...!

Journaling is similar but different, in that by writing down problems and the thoughts and feelings associated with them, you gain a deeper understanding of yourself, see yourself clearer and relieve both physical and emotional tension by putting it on paper. You literally get to read your own mind and that can be immensely therapeutic. Journaling is an internal processing method that brings peace, healing and ends confusion.

More than that, science has proved that by writing about emotionally difficult things that are going on in your life for 20 minutes a day, for three or four days, your immune system gets stronger. Releasing the tension by writing about it directly affects your physical capacity to remain healthy under stress.

Journaling has been proven to be very beneficial in helping you to understand yourself and the issues you face so that eventually you'll be able to recognize problems that stem from them.

Journaling can be used in times of grief and loss, to help you cope with a life-changing diagnosis and trauma, to strengthen relationships, communication or self-esteem, and can also help you to see the bigger picture. It's a wonderful tool.

Not too sure about grammar and spelling? Who cares; what

matters is honest and authentic content.

It's also a good bench-marking tool – if you start a journal today, noting down your feelings and how you think the exercises are working, day by day you make these notes. Then in six months time you read back over your writing and you will see how far you have come, and how changes have affected your life. It will also prove this to you: when you imagine yourself in the future, you will not be the person you are now.

When I started my first journal, I decided to name it Clio after the Greek muse of historical poetry. Perhaps you'd like to go and find a special note-book; or a look, a color, size or something else that matters to you. Who knows, perhaps a padlock...

Note to Self

While you have pen and paper to hand, would you like to consider some letter writing – or some notes? Reminders and to-do lists are OK too.

Good days and bad days are just days that you experience differently and if you were to evaluate a bad day from the perspective of a good day, it may even seem like you were a different person on that bad day. The same goes for happy and sad days.

But today is a good day – you're in control, you love life and know how to deal with setbacks, self-talk that holds you back, and doubts about your abilities. So if you were to look at the person you are on a bad day, what would you write on the 'Note to Self'?

Right now, write a note or a letter to yourself, to be read on a bad day. Write from the heart with compassion and encouragement – if self-love and caring for yourself doesn't feel comfortable yet, write it as if to your best friend. What would you do for them? Make them smile? Offer practical support or advice? Tell them they're worth more, deserve better and things will look different in the morning? Perhaps all of these? Add some reminders of particularly good moments when you excelled and nothing could make you come down from the top of the world.

So start writing with loving care, because you are that best friend, you deserve better, and when things seem a little darker, when you feel like there is nobody in the entire world who understands what you feel and what you're going through, pull out the letter and read it over and over again. Maybe your inner critic will resist, determined to keep you in the void of gloom, but for just one moment let go of the destructive thoughts, just breathe and be. Everything else can wait a little and you can reach for the good feelings; how you felt as you wrote the letter, what had happened to make it such a good day. One feeling, one thought and one memory at a time will gradually restore balance and you'll come to believe that things will look better in the morning.

How about compassionate days? The days when you are flexible and unconditional enough to not be bothered by the small stuff, when your philosophy is 'live and let live.' Would that be a good time to write a letter of forgiveness to yourself? Or perhaps to forgive someone for what they did to you, whether it was yesterday or many years ago.

A harsh fact of unforgiveness is that the only person who suffers is you. Hurt, pain, betrayal, abuse or trauma – unless you let it go, it will happen to you for the rest of your life. To forgive someone else is to set yourself free. They will no longer have a hold on you, can't terrorize your mind and thoughts, and you'll be able to move your life forward in more ways than one – with newfound strength and confidence. Oh, and did I mention that the same goes for self-forgiveness?

Exercise: Imagine That

Imagine you are walking down a winding path towards a warm secluded beach. You can see the bright orange sun in the midst of a clear blue sky. Its golden rays shimmer on the sea and the beach seems to stretch for miles. As you step onto the sand it feels warm beneath your feet. It is totally peaceful apart from the sound of each wave breaking and you watch as one wave breaks on top of the other. There is a cool breeze and you take three deep breaths in. You can smell the salty water and taste the salt on your lips. As you sit down on the sand, you look up into the sky when you hear the noise of seagulls as they glide overhead. Then you notice the clouds floating across the deep blue color that joins with the sea. Take a few moments to watch the clouds and see the different shapes they make. Then focus on the waves slowly ebbing and flowing onto the shore. Lie down on the sand and as you feel the warm sun on your skin, start to focus on your breath as you breathe in and out.

Imagine then that you suddenly feel a part of you rising above your body and heading towards the clouds in the sky, until you feel you are sitting on a soft, comfortable cloud looking down on yourself. Your body lying on the beach seems so small from this distance. Take a moment to relax and look around at the panoramic view. You can see the beach, and the sea and cliffs surrounding it. Take a deep breath of the salty air. When you are ready, gently float back into your body on the beach. As you slowly get up and walk back towards the rough pathway you feel a deep sense of peace. Take another deep breath before you open your eyes.

14 Happiness

Aristotle observed that we choose virtues like honor, pleasure, reason and gratitude not just for themselves, but to be happy. He also noticed that we never choose happiness to acquire the virtues and so concluded that Happiness is a self-sufficient emotion.

But what is it, really?

First, let's clarify that there are two distinct types of happiness; the transient feeling that you get in the moment and the more permanent ongoing feeling of well-being and satisfaction. We're focusing on the latter.

Let's go back to Aristotle and his notion of what constitutes a 'good life,' and the positive emotions like cheerfulness, serenity, joy, optimism, gratitude and kindness that make us happy. There are some things in particular that contribute to the feeling:

- Contributing to society – whether it's volunteering your time, or being active in local groups or communities.
- Having a wider social circle of friends and a sense of belonging in your local community.
- Giving and receiving healthy attention without judgment.
- Having a sense of control over what happens in your life. There are many things you can't control, so being clear about the areas where you do have a say is both empowering and liberating.
- Close unconditional friendships.
- Intimacy, family, partners.
- Personal growth and achievements.
- Recognizing purpose and meaning in life.

True happiness is not about possessions or money – or anything else external for that matter. It comes from inside you. Let me tell you a story of happiness:

In my work with past life regression, my clients are taken through the death of a previous life and given the opportunity to reflect on what important lessons they can bring with them to the present life. Over the years I have regressed many hundreds of people and they all have the same to say:

- I wish I had spent more time with the people I loved.
- I wish I hadn't worried so much.
- I wish I'd said 'I love you' more often to the people that mattered.
- I wish I hadn't worked so hard.
- I wish I hadn't been so pre-occupied with making money and getting material things.
- I wish I had spent more time being happy.

Without fail I hear the same sentiment expressed over and over again. I often get letters and emails some months after the sessions when life has become easier, and many people tell me they understand the purpose of life better and feel a lot happier.

One client who had tried to conceive for a long time was pregnant within three months of going back in time; I still don't know what issues she resolved, but it worked for her.

14 Rules of Happiness

1 Stop being a victim – take back whatever control you can, this includes being informed of your choices, voicing your opinion and being heard.
2 Be grateful – for everything and everyone you have in your life right now.
3 Say 'Yes' with pleasure and 'No' without worries.
4 Start the journey towards your bliss, your dream. Go where you feel happy.
5 Learn to let go – of emotional baggage that serves no purpose apart from slowing you down, and realise that you are not your emotions.
6 Practice acts of kind gestures randomly – a smile, holding the door open for someone, giving up a seat or telling someone you care about them. The best thing about giving is that it makes you feel so very happy, costs nothing and has incredible rippling effects. Do one act every day for a week and at the weekend reflect on the difference.
7 Be in the moment – because that's all we have – the present. The past and the future are just other moments, but you live in the present one. Holding on to the past or looking to the future stops you from experiencing the present. An abundance of happiness awaits you Right Now. Be here and feel it.
8 Clear out the stuff – material things never bring lasting happiness. Make space in your life. Then, enroll in a belly-dancing class and have some fun.
9 Spend time with friends – people with larger social networks are happier and more successful.
10 Get some love in your life – and give a little more to those close to you.

11 Work in some simplicity – slow down; go for a walk in a park or in the countryside. Create simple rituals that make you feel good; do them often.

12 Accept what is right now – spending time fighting and resisting is futile and a breeding ground for anger and depression. Acceptance brings peace and possible change.

13 Care for your body – your body is designed to be active and your digestive system is perfectly made for a well-balanced, natural diet.

14 The last rule is actually two of my favorite sayings: love like you've never been hurt; dance like nobody's watching.

Lastly, the two things that can make you very unhappy...

TV

Consumerism

Exercise: Imagine That

Just relaxing, going back in time to a memory of being on a beach or by a river bank. The ocean or a lake perhaps.

Now you know of course that being on a beach, you find water and sand. Perhaps you can imagine that now. I don't know if you can, but if you do, you'll be hearing the sound of the water. Waves slowly rolling in from the sea maybe. The sun glistening off the water and the waves, its rays warming your shoulders and your face. Underfoot you'll feel the sand, warm on the soles of your feet. If you dig your toes down in the sand, you'll feel the coolness as your feet burrow down in the wet sand.

Above, seagulls are calling and hovering on the wing and you can watch them glide effortlessly on the wind, as the waves rise and fall, rolling onto the sand with that lazy lapping sound you get on calm days.

A seagull lands on the beach, close to the water's edge just as the wave retreats, and you can see the reflection in the sand. As the bird starts walking towards you it seem to be changing shape, transforming, becoming larger and almost all gray now.

As it comes closer to you, the beak grows and changes; a nose and a horn appear. Deep inside you know what's coming now, so just allow the rhinoceros to stand there, waves lapping at its feet. Watch those waves moving in and out in a comfortable, easy motion, so relaxing, at the feet of the rhino.

Notice how it actually fits into your beach scene, if you introduce it one step at a time – however incredible it may seem.

15 Small Miracles

Lifestyles often don't offer many opportunities for us to see the miracles in everyday things or moments. Work, social life, stress, worries, tiredness and frustration all take their toll. As do apathy and hopelessness. It's easy to contemplate giving up when forces seem to conspire against you.

What I'd like to introduce are the four phrases that can make your world shift sideways for the better.

Understanding that nobody else is to blame and you are not to blame. Things just are. Stop blaming yourself, taking on the responsibility for things you couldn't possibly have control over. *That*, you have control over, *that*, you are responsible for. You can stop, and it is your responsibility to stop. Be kind to yourself.

Life, when we really look at it, is full of miracles and we are too busy to notice or pay attention, so now is the time to sit up straight and give a moment to the little wonders surrounding you.

'I am sorry' – say this to yourself quietly and with compassion. 'I am sorry.' You've been hard on yourself, asked so much of your mind, your body and probably berated more that you have praised. Take responsibility for ending this, be responsible for the kindness you deserve, be in control of giving this to yourself. Love yourself more, accept yourself more.

'Forgive me' – give compassion, love and care to the inner you who has always been there and seldom been heard, whose needs have been ignored and hardly ever been allowed to come out to play.

'I love you' – this is a good thing to say as you look at yourself in the mirror. Self-love, self-care and generosity for your strengths and weaknesses create space and ability to love others for who they are without conditions or judgment. Thinking loving thoughts has immediate and healing results.

'Thank you' – the simplest phrase of them all. It shows gratitude that you listened to yourself and paid attention to the other three phrases.

Next time you prepare vegetables or pick up a piece of fruit, give a thought to the fact that what you're holding in your hand is mostly sunshine. A seed, soil, some water and sunshine that miraculously becomes an apple or a pepper.

When you look at nature or gaze out over a vast expanse of water and think it's beautiful, it's you who create the magic. Nature doesn't strive to be beautiful, it just is what it is – the beauty you ascribe it comes from you.

Childhood memories can be filled with the awe and wonder of those innocent years; just think back to those days and the miracles will come flooding back.

Days that lasted for years, moments that went by in a flash, visits to the seaside; if you think back to days out when you were a child, I bet you can still taste the food you had.

Or in the words of a teenager I know:

'Isn't paint brilliant – all those colors!'

16 Deer in the Headlights

Remember I told you that you can read this book in any order as long as you read the initial chapters first? I lied. Which is why this chapter is towards the end, because the benefits from it are greater if you have read and done some of the exercises in the other chapters.

There are a few components to this thought and it all leads to a powerful visualization that will invigorate and enliven your senses!

In the chapter Introducing Stress, I talked about 'fight, flight or freeze' – the age-old instinctive reaction to a threatening situation.

   If you think about 'freeze' as the deer in the headlights, the 'play possum' or 'roll over and play dead' behavior, this is the way you feel when you are faced with a dangerous situation. 'I just froze and couldn't move,' is something people often say when describing what it was like being really scared. They say similar things when they have been told something unpleasant, devastating or life-changing; 'I felt numb, frozen; I couldn't even open my mouth to speak.'

   Think back over your life, there may be moments when you froze – perhaps diagnoses delivered by doctors, even insensitive comments made by medical staff, friends or colleagues – any comment that made your body react like a 'deer in the headlights,' any time in your life. When you remember, the feeling of freezing up will flood your system again, because the impact of the words was so strong it's like an imprint on your cells and your reaction is the same now as then.

Now, let's move to another component:

74

Masaru Emoto wrote a book called *Hidden Messages in Water* which is a real eye opener:

He has photographed water crystals where the water has been exposed to different words before freezing; beautifully-shaped crystals when water hears loving, empowering or healing words; and broken mis-shaped crystals when the words are hurtful and negative. You'll find some of the photos on the Internet and I have included a link in the Resource section.

And finally, add this part:

Your body is made up of at least 50% water. The fact that the symmetry and beauty of water can only be seen when it freezes to ice crystals has more to do with liquids and solids, the states of matter, and that it's easier to distinguish the shape of a frozen drop of water.

Water that is in its liquid form is in constant flux and the crystal shape is dependant on the words it is exposed to immediately before freezing. So...

The comment 'I just froze on the spot,' includes the water in your body and how it took on a broken, misaligned and negative shape. The words we use are sometimes closer to the truth than we think.

Your cells remember, remember?

Set your heart and mind to Defrost and warm your frozen feelings with this:

Exercise: Imagine That

You know you can relax as deeply as you want, anytime you want. So just go to that soft and gentle place when you're ready in your own time and space.

When you feel ready to close your eyes, go ahead and enter the blissful inner world where right in front of you on the floor is a circle of light – just as bright as you can imagine a circle of light to be. You may notice that you can step into the circle, and when you do the light makes a sound, a sort of humming, like a vibration. It's so relaxing and you feel so serene standing in the circle where amazing things can happen and wonderful journeys can be had.

But right now you focus on any trauma that made you freeze, made you powerless and fearful. Just think about it, and feel exactly where in your body it took root. Now the circle is slowly moving upward, healing and warming your body along the way. Just experience the warmth, the tingling sensation as every cell, every muscle, your bones and tissues change, and every organ including your blood flow is healed and re-generated, repaired and re-awakened as the circle slowly moves up your body. When it reaches the spot you identified you may feel a slight jolt, like a mild electric shock, as negative turns to positive and your cells are imprinted with new healthy information.

Let the circle go right to the top of your head, feel its healing energy all the way and as it stops for a brief moment before returning to the floor, use that moment to notice the change in your body. As the circle moves back down you feel the healing vibrations where there is still healing to be done.

When the circle is back on the floor you can step out of it and back into the room you are in. Sit a while and reflect on the experience. You can return as often as you feel the need.

17. The Hero's Journey

You've come a long way, from the beginning of the book to this point. Now you can think back on all the ideas you've had, the inspiration and realization about you, your journey and place in the world; so now you're near the end. Of this book and this journey, at least. In some sense it's just the beginning – even if you decide to stay just where you are, to be exactly who you are for a while longer, because that's fine too. I hope you picked up the message that runs through every chapter: you're just fine. You're not broken.

Putting it All Together

If you have read every page of the book or flicked through and found one or two ideas that made you stop, perhaps so briefly that you didn't even register it, you'll be ready and very able to complete the final stage. However, some problems, or facts that we have to face, are too big to acknowledge and it's easier to pretend that everything is fine. As long as we don't talk about it, nobody will notice the elephant in the room. Somewhere in the back of your mind you know that sooner or later you have to deal with it, but as long as you don't mention it to anyone, perhaps it'll just go away, cease to be a problem. It's like a bad secret – if you keep it inside, it festers and grows until it becomes an all-consuming beast that you fear more than anything else. You wake up in the morning and for a brief second all is well; until your thoughts remind you of the reality. It's like the unspoken secret or problem has some power over you; it takes away joy, happiness and integrity and makes you distant from those who would help and support – it makes everything seem impossible. There's no way out and there is no solution. Or maybe...speaking the words, accepting that you have a problem to solve is the first step in a positive direction and as soon as you do, you'll notice that whatever you thought had control over you just lost all power.

Travelling Companions

Telling a story as it is, either in a journal or in a letter or to someone you know who will listen without judgment or comment, will shine a light on your story, your words. Any words that diminish your experience or invalidate your feelings can't be used; there is just no place for them. Tell it like it is; what you know, what you learned, what you feel, where you're at right now, where you have been, where you'd like to be, describing any obstacle that's stopping at the moment. Above all don't miss out painful or embarrassing facts or cover up details you find hard to say out loud. Clarity and honesty will take you to an extraordinary place where you first feel the lightness of being, free from the internal turmoil and gradually become able to put some distance between yourself and the problem. It becomes manageable, less threatening and you can see it for what it really is. It's likely that other people play a part and they'll have their share of the problem to deal with; you're responsible for yourself, no one else. As you recall feelings and facts, you'll begin to see what part each person, including you, played in the events that have lead to this point. There is no blame, no blaming, just facts. That way you avoid all the bitterness and resentment that goes hand in hand with the blame game. So take your friend or your journal and come along to the next step on this magical mystery tour.

Now you know where the problem came from, you've put it squarely in the spotlight and you know that the only person who can remove it from your life is you. At this point you may become really aware of wanting to cut the ties that have held you captive.

Do you want to make the symbolic cutting a little more real? With a pair of scissors at hand get a length of cord or string and tie it around your left wrist (right wrist if you're left-handed). Close your eyes and start thinking about your decision to solve the problem; think about your resourcefulness and resolve. At the moment you feel empowered, ready to move on – cut the cord and notice the shift inside.

Without the warming and life-giving light of the sun, there would be no shadows, no dark corners in a well-lit room. Shadows are of course nothing more than a reflection of an object or a person who is standing between you and the light. One way of dealing with this is to re-position yourself so that you can see everything clearly and be warm at the same time. There are some shadows that appear from time to time, just when you've got comfortable they creep in without you really noticing, but the more clearing you do, the easier it will be to spot and deal with them.

Anger is a powerful feeling that's often suppressed or pushed back down, so when you stop trying to please everyone else but yourself, it will come to the surface time and again. Rejecting or denying it only serves to make you feel paralyzed, trapped by an inertia that makes you blame others and feel like a victim. It implodes; your anger turns to hatred and bitterness that shades everything in black and various shades of gray that eventually seep into your heart and soul. You, being the clever person that you are, know how to bring it all out in the open, take the power away from the negative emotions, deal with it appropriately and move on shrouded in an air of rainbow colors. Perhaps you'll even find compassion for the person or the event that angered you. Maybe you'll be the strong one who forgives?

Being afraid, living with fear, is more of an existence where you have retreated into yourself, afraid of showing who you really are. If you sit still, if you stay silent, perhaps no one will notice you, right? Despite your fear a seed of courage grows inside, the wish to be seen and heard; to be recognized as a person who deserves to be respected and noticed. Some thought of 'if I don't do it now, it'll be too late' may cross your mind. That thought is a passionate call from your soul, to stand up, be counted and make your mark in the world.

Let's get back to a part of anger; hatred, to be precise. I am always saddened when I hear people speak about former spouses and how bitterness and hate is felt for years after the event. If your relationship is over, let it be over and done with; let it go. Hatred ties you to the past, to the person and every time you allow those emotions to surface you'll relive the initial pain. I can almost guarantee that the only person suffering is you. The one you 'hate' is probably not even aware of it. Sometimes the choices you have are whether to live in the present creating a bright future, or whether to hang on to something that is just a memory and will never be a reality. There is a similarity between this hatred and the anger you can feel towards someone close who dies. The difference is that you usually learn to grieve for someone who's no longer alive, but it's not so easy to do the same if you confuse your ex-spouse with the object of the sadness– the relationship – which is dead. Once you learn to grieve for that you'll be on your way to letting go, feeling happier and much more confident.

There is a form of guilt that comes from wanting to please everyone but there is another guilt that occurs when you have compromised your values. When you have acted in such a way that your behavior goes against everything you stand for and believe in. I dislike gossip, particularly when it involves people who aren't there and what is being said isn't very kind. Many years ago, I worked in an office where gossip was rife, but I managed to avoid being drawn into the conversations until a new co-worker started in the office – and we just didn't get on. One day I felt particularly irritated and guess what...yes, I vented my feelings behind her back. Afterwards I felt really bad – not necessarily for the other person, but bad that I'd done it at all. I might as well have stolen money from all of them or lied about them; I had devalued everything I believed in, everything I still stand for. That kind of guilt needs to be faced; whatever you did needs to be rectified, for your own peace of mind and integrity.

Occasionally I meet people who refuse to deal with any of the issues mentioned so far. They are in denial, they express passionate anger that points a blaming finger towards victims and assailants alike; and then suddenly they become very subdued, as if all energy has left and only exhaustion remains. It takes a lot of energy to run away from that which is always there as soon as you stop to think. It becomes an all-consuming purpose of life; to not live it, just to avoid it by any means possible.

Time out and a fresh perspective will re-energize and invigorate you. Do something fun, laugh; be brave and do something that scares you; read an indulgent book, do something extraordinary to transform the ordinary. Chances are you'll look at your problem with fresh eyes and the mountain will look more like a hill.

What if you don't? What if instead you jump feet first into the black hole of capitulation and believe that there are no solutions and no answers to your plight? Do one thing for yourself: keep an open mind. What have you got to lose? If you feel so overwhelmed and exhausted that you are without answers, you can stop fighting. Allow support and ideas to come to you instead. In this place you can let go – perhaps even without fear of what will happen if you do, because somewhere you passed the point of it making a difference. I'd like you to know that incredible things can happen when you face your personal event horizon.

Exercise: Imagine That

It can be so pleasant to just let go, do nothing; daydream perhaps. To just let your mind wander, let your body relax. Zoning out, listening in and hearing sounds that surround. Cars, rain, high heels on the pavement or children telling the story of their day at school. Noises in shops, the endless beep-beep at the check-out. And the times you just went in there for a couple of things and didn't bother with a basket but when you're in the queue, your arms are full of all the extra stuff; it's heavy, your arms ache but if you move you'll probably drop it all. Can you feel the relief as you put everything down and the muscles in your arms can relax? You watch as all the things you decided to buy are moving forward, beep-beep, and then you have to pick it all up again and carry it home. Remember what a relief it is when you finally come home, put the bags down, breathe in, breathe out and relax. That's the moment you can zone out, take five and just not bother doing anything until you have found new energy. The bags of shopping are still there, everything waits for you while you take a rest. Now you don't need to juggle everything at once, worry that everything will fall out of your hands. One thing at a time; unpack, put it where it belongs. Breathing out with a sense of satisfaction that you did it, you carried all that weight, you didn't drop or break a single thing and now everything is sorted, you can relax and you know exactly where you've put things. So now, as you have remembered all that, you can just lean back, be comfortable with your feeling of satisfaction in knowing that, when needed, you can balance a lot of things at once and place them exactly where they need to be.

What's it All About Anyway?

Have you noticed that some things come back over and over again? Mistakes and choices you make can be the wrong ones – in partners, jobs and anything from the food you order in the restaurant to the friendships you make. It seems fine in the beginning, but suddenly you recognize the signs and just as you freeze on the spot, you have time to think, 'I've been here before.' It's like the universe has conspired to present the same scenario time and again until you get it and understand the significance of the lesson. Then and only then can you move on. Is there any way to avoid having bad habits rubbed in your face? I think you know the answer, but I have a pleasant surprise for you – shortcuts. The first instance you recognize a life lesson in the making, take action and move on. It may be a habit that you've outgrown and need to move away from; or a trait that needs attention and correction. Or it may be lifestyles and choices that your body is asking you to stop or change; the inner voice can deliver the lesson too. Perhaps the most uncomfortable notion is that you actually created the situation; unwittingly you made the choice that has become wrong or destructive. Give some thought to it; what do you gain from it? A client wanted to understand why she always ended up in relationships with very needy men, always becoming the one who organized, carried, supported, cooked and cuddled according to their needs. Looking at something from a distance can help you see things differently. You see the whole picture, not the details. This client soon realized that her choice made her feel totally capable; it enabled her to ignore her own weakness, and not until she dealt with this would she be able to establish a healthier, more equal relationship.

If you discover that it's a habit like smoking or eating too much of the wrong stuff, try this:

With your eyes closed, imagine a grid of squares in front of you. It can be a simple grid with black or white lines, or something far more sci-fi like the green glowing squares from *The Matrix*. When you can picture it, bring to mind something you really like to eat – or if it's smoking, think of why you like it and create a symbol for it. Let your picture float onto the grid; it will find its own place, so just observe where it is. Now, think of something you really dislike – something that you can't imagine eating or even putting in your mouth. Make the experience very real; see yourself close to it, smelling it, and a piece of it ending up in your mouth...and see where on the grid this revolting item is placed. Take your 'like' item and place it on the 'dislike' item so it covers it. This is how I stopped eating chocolate...

I'd like to make a diversion here, because sometimes it's not absolutely clear why one part of you wants to keep on doing what the other part would like to change.

Look into My Eyes

Relaxing, putting the demands of the world on hold for a short while and turning your attention to the inner world is usually all it takes to create changes in thoughts and feelings. I read somewhere that if we visualize doing something over and over again, it becomes much easier to actually do it. Ahead of a driving test it would be useful to visualize driving a car, performing all the maneuvers; changing gears, signalling, braking...in fact, closing your eyes and imaging a relaxed and successful driving lesson repeatedly will help you prepare for the exam day with less trepidation – and very likely pass the test.

There are times when a deeper state of being will be much more beneficial and self-hypnosis is an excellent skill to possess. Like all other tools and skills you'll learn in this book, it can be used for a multitude of reasons, at all times for all things you deem necessary. Hypnosis has got a slightly negative reputation and a lot of myths have been spun around it. Although what you'll learn here is simple self-hypnosis, let's clear up a few misconceptions:

- Nobody can make you do things against your will. If you've seen someone volunteer to be on stage and cluck like a chicken or forget their own name, bear in mind that deep down they wanted a moment of fame, whatever it took to get it.
- You can't get stuck in a trance anymore than you can get stuck in sleep or in a daydream. You may find it so pleasant that you'd like to extend the experience a little longer than intended, but all that will ever happen is that you'll be so relaxed that you'll fall asleep and wake up fresh and energized.
- On the subject of sleep – hypnosis is not sleep. It's a heightened state of awareness when your focus is narrowed down to just a few things. You don't forget what happens or what is said to you. Perhaps a few things will slip out of your memory, but how often can you recall any conversation verbatim?
- What if the house is on fire and you're in a trance? Open your eyes. That's really all you have to do to break the trance state and deal with the fire or any other emergency for that matter. The same applies at any point when you want to get back to the external reality – just open your eyes look around the room and shake yourself into action. It's just like when you're reading a good book or watching something on TV that has all your attention and the phone rings. You snap back to the room and answer the phone. How many times have you driven somewhere and as you reach your destination, you wonder how you got there because your mind was on other things. If anything unusual or untoward was to occur, you'd be fully alert

again – just as in the trance you'll experience when you're not driving.

Of course there are different levels of hypnosis, from light trance to somnambulism, but we're going to stay somewhere around the light to mid-depth of trance. Considering that you go in and out of a trance at least a couple of times everyday, it only becomes complicated when you start thinking about how to do it, rather than just doing it.

If you have an internal battle – be it with nicotine, food, relationships, money or anything that causes you to think, 'why do I keep doing this?' – then remember that the subconscious is in charge and it only does what it thinks is good for you, based on the first time you did what you no longer want to do, however misguided. Getting a dialogue going between your two parts is a way of understanding why one part wants to keep up the behavior, and, importantly, when you are in a trance it's easier to get an agreement for change, or to reach a compromise that's acceptable for both sides.

Exercise: Imagine That

You know how to imagine things, how the mind can make pictures, stories – and you know how to relax and let go of mundane thoughts. Right now, you don't have to be anywhere or do anything else, just imagine images. You can imagine or picture an elevator; large, roomy, peaceful and silent with a soft, thick carpet that mutes your steps as you walk in and gentle golden lighting that makes everything look as if it's bathed in the light of the setting sun, making you feel warm and comfortable. As the doors close with an almost imperceptible sound, you look up above the door where the floor numbers are displayed. As you stand there, comfortable, relaxed with nothing in particular demanding your attention, the elevator starts moving down. It's funny, how even if you can't really see it moving, you can get a sensation of the downward movement, particularly as you look up at the numbers above the door, watching them change. You can probably see them in your mind, the light changing from 10 to 9 to 8 and with every change you feel your body sinking further down into a peaceful relaxed place – safe; 7 makes you feel deeply relaxed, 6, 5, counting all the numbers, seeing all the shapes down to 0. Now the door opens and in front of you is an open fire and an easy chair – it's your favorite chair to sit in when you want to rest. Have a seat, feel the warmth from the fire; perhaps you'll also notice a faint smell of pine from the log gently burning in the fireplace. When you're feeling so at ease it's easy to think about the part of you that won't change. The one who wants to smoke, the one who hates exercise or adores chocolate – so bring that part out into the open now, put it in your hand and notice if it's in the left or the right hand. Is it male or female? Old or young? Angry, happy, frightened? Notice every detail. It's such a comfortable chair you're in and if you need to move to be even more comfortable, just shift your body until you almost feel as if you're sinking into the chair. There, just perfect; just a deep sigh of contentment. This is the time for discussion, asking the part you have in your hand what it wants for you – because you understand that it just wants what's best for you.

So go ahead and ask and listen very carefully to the answer. When you have a better understanding of why you do things, it becomes easier to find a middle ground, a compromise or a deal that will be acceptable to both parts of you. Answers can come in many forms – sometimes a picture, a song, just a single word or a memory from long ago explains things completely and you now have the opportunity to find out how you can change without the fight. You're just too comfortable, the fire warming your face and hands; notice how warm and cozy your feet are. Now I'd like you to imagine in front of you a bridge, a bridge over a small stream or just a bridge in a landscaped garden that leads you from flowerbeds to shady trees. Stepping onto the bridge you'll feel how strong and safe it is, the handrails made from wrought iron feel cool against your warm skin, and the wooden planks underfoot seem thick and solid. As you look across the bridge the part of you that you held in your hand is standing waiting, crossing the bridge exactly at the same time as you. It's like walking towards a friend, someone you have known for a very long time, so a smile forms on your lips and you're greeted with the same friendly smile. You are meeting a friend you love and trust right on the middle of the bridge. One idea of a greeting to your friend could be, 'I love you very much and I want you to change. Together we can do it and be much happier and healthier. What do you say?' This is meeting halfway, understanding that love is the source of both the old and the new. When you reach an agreement, embrace the part of you that has learned something so important and feel how the two of you become one. It's a relief and it's exciting to know that now you can make changes for the better; it's so good you don't really mind leaving the comfortable chair by the fireside. Walk back into the elevator; it's there waiting for you. As you step in and the door glides closed, you focus on the numbers above the door again as you feel the elevator moving upward. 10, 9, 8 – you see the numbers in your mind; 7, 6, as you feel more awake, more alert; 5, 4, like you've had a long restful sleep; 3,2, and now you are wide awake, refreshed and 1, feeling ready to get on with your day.

Reflection and honesty, however uncomfortable, may provide you with an answer or course of action to take. By looking inward and listening to the voice of intuition, being still and allowing it to happen, you will get a sense of how truly amazing you really are. Be prepared for an insight, a flash in a moment shorter than a heartbeat –once felt, never forgotten.

You may be tempted to shake off old restricting values, try new ideas and create beauty that resonates with the core of your being. A painting or a poem, new colors, tastes, smells or sounds; you find yourself humming along to your own tune. As you begin to clear out all the beliefs that you inherited from someone else, and as you begin to question your reason for bowing to pressure that serves no purpose, a space is made for new, better and enriching experiences and truths. And this time, when you believe in something, when you attain a value, it really is yours: your truth, your voice. In the beginning you may feel vulnerable speaking it out loud; it is after all a piece of you, your innermost being that's brought out into the open. Practice! Speak it often, with courage and conviction, and before you know it you'll become aware of how right it feels to do so.

If you painted a picture or wrote a poem, I'm sure it will reflect some part of your transformation. Most definitely, if you look in the mirror, you'll see it in your eyes.

Being Wabi-Sabi

If you have ever held a piece of driftwood, or a pebble that you picked on a beach, you know how smooth they are, how time, sand, water and wind have shaped them. If you have observed a flower from bud to bloom or sat on a riverbank and been mesmerized by the dancing rivulets of water flowing and felt the beauty that develops between you and the object, you have experienced wabi-sabi. Japanese Zen Buddhists in the 12th century performed wabi-sabi in the tea ceremony by observing every movement, every step involved, respecting and honoring the ceremony. Let me enlighten your path with my wabi-sabi love for you:

It is simple, the beauty of nature and the world around you, the changing tides and seasons – each has a beauty to be observed. When you become aware, your mind and soul move the universe with energy and awareness of the transience of everything and everybody. Nothing lasts forever, nothing is ever finished and nothing is perfect – and so they have their own perfect imperfection. Love the imperfection in yourself, the passing of time and the changes that it brings to you, those around you and the material things you surround yourself with. Go with the flow, accept the changes and don't fight them.

You and I are the custodians of this Earth for the generations yet to come – they too will question, be confused, hurt, laugh, love and fear just as you do. They will look for answers, have quests and questions and find the courage to transcend their fears and barriers – just like you.

The important things are being true to yourself, being happy with who you are and trusting your intuition; being content, enjoying life for what it is and what you feel is most important to you in your life. Expressing your true self in harmony with your values, knowing that passion and happiness come from deep within, not from material possessions or at the expense of others. And like the tree in the wind, be flexible, adapt to change and relish in the new challenges it brings. Observe the imperfections and transience in those you love; allow them their opportunity to change and they will love you all the more for it. You were never broken, you were always perfect and you were always loved. Just like you are now.

The Power of Three

Think of three ideas, skills or experiences you have tried or developed since starting to read this book, writing or reflecting on:

- how you felt before you gained the new wisdom
- how you felt while learning it
- how things have changed since bringing it into your everyday life

Sometimes we pick up ideas and concepts without really noticing and unless you shine a light on them and bring attention to your new skills, you may think you didn't learn anything at all. So now that you're aware of how subtly things can slip into the subconscious mind and just blend in, it would be a good time to decide on the next three changes or skills you want to incorporate:

- Write down the three new skills you have decided to learn.
- Explain how they will make a difference or how they will enhance what you already know.
- Write the story or play the movie of how your life will be then.

Remember to always

Let Life Live Through You

'There is a vitality, a life force, a quickening that is translated through you into action, and there is only one of you in all time, this expression is unique, and if you block it, it will never exist through any other medium; it will be lost. The world will not have it. It is not your business to determine how good it is, nor how it compares with another expression. It is your business to keep it yours clearly and directly, to keep the channel open. You do not even have to believe in yourself or your work. You have to keep open and aware directly to the urges that motivate you. Keep the channel open. No artist is pleased. There is no satisfaction whatever at any time. There is only a queer, divine dissatisfaction, a blessed unrest that keeps us marching and makes us more alive than the others.'

(Martha Graham)

Resources

There are so many wonderful, inspiring books, websites and people that can take you to the next level. Here are some that I think will be particularly worthy of your time:

Mindfulness:
Mindfulness for Dummies
    Author: Shamash Alidina
    www.learnmindfulness.co.uk
Reconciliation: Healing the Inner Child
    Author: Thich Nhat Hanhn

Relaxation:
The Relaxation Response
    Author: Herbert Benson

Guided Imagery:
Belleruth Naparstek's Guided Imagery Centre
www.healthjourneys.com

Personal Development:
Awareness Engineering and other fantastic things
    www.maryleelabay.com
You Can Be Amazing
    Author: Ursula James

Food for thought:
The Hidden Messages in Water
    Author: Masaru Emoto

Most of the authors have written and published many more books and are available on Amazon in all countries.

AYNI
BOOKS

"Ayni" is a Quechua word meaning "reciprocity" – sharing, giving and receiving - whatever you give out comes back to you. To be in Ayni is to be in balance, harmony and right relationship with oneself and nature, of which we are all an intrinsic part. Complementary and Alternative approaches to health and well-being essentially follow a holistic model, within which one is given support and encouragement to move towards a state of balance, true health and wholeness, ultimately leading to the awareness of one's unique place in the Universal jigsaw of life – Ayni, in fact.